GU00786361

# Let's Pop Culture!
## o(^0^)o

## A guide to Japanese culture by real Japanese high school students

Contributions by Sendai Mukaiyama high school students. Edited by Matthew Rowe

ISBN: 1482072505
ISBN-13: 978-1482072501

# A BIG THANK YOU

This book was produced with the help of funds raised at IndieGoGo, a popular crowdsourcing site and community, whom without which this book would not be possible.

All the students and teachers at Mukaiyama High school would like to express their deepest thanks for the opportunity IndieGoGo gave us, to the backers who generously donated money to our publication and to every person who helped spread word of our unique and pioneering project.

Those backers are (in alphabetical order):

*Jamie Anderson, Rhys Anslow, Tyler Ellis, Andrew Goldman, Lewis Hill, Shin Kato, Yoshinori Mori, Kei Moriya, Liam Stubbs, and all those who wish to remain anonymous.*

Thank you so much! You have made it possible for our students to feel confident about their English ability and for them to help neighboring disaster victims. Thank you.

We would also like to thank Amazon Createspace for the opportunity to publish our own work; Shogakukan, Shopro, Culture Japan and Danny Choo, Alodia Gosiengfiao and their photographers for use of their images, our Principal, Mr. Ono Hidetoshi for agreeing to the project; all the supporters on Twitter and our Facebook page; and you... yes, you, because you bought the book, didn't you?

# CONTENTS

Japanese culture has already spread far around the world and is popular for many reasons in many different countries. Most people know what a 'samurai' or a 'ninja' is from movies and cartoons. People have long enjoyed the hilarious stylings from the disparate likes of Godzilla and Japanese game shows too.

How many people reading this book now used to stay up late to watch poor chumps slip off bizarre obstacle courses and otherwise humiliate themselves in *Takeshi's Castle*? How many of you have seen or been to a sushi restaurant? No, don't raise your hands. I can't see you. Children could probably tell you about *Pokemon*, and *Naruto* and *Evangelion* because 'anime', or animation, is one of Japan's biggest exports, one with a whole subculture of its own. Yet, Japan still remains one of the most mysterious cultures to outsiders.

©藤子プロ・小学館・テレビ朝日・シンエイ・ADK

There are still many parts of the Japanese culture that go undiscovered and will surprise you when you get here. For example, speaking of anime, I had no idea what *Doraemon* was before I came to Japan, because we just don't have it at all in the UK. However it's an incredibly huge anime franchise in Japan. His (for it is a character) cultural equivalent might be Mickey Mouse or Snoopy. You might also think you are pretty "nihon savy" if you know of the movie director Beat Takeshi. Yet, even if you know of his often violent and dark gangster movies, you might be surprised to learn that in Japan he is best known for being a slapstick comedian! It's a bizarre twist.

That's why there are people who, immersed in Japan's culture, then do their best to introduce it to the world. If you have been interested in Japan for a while, there is a good chance that you will know about Danny Choo.

He's quite a prominent ambassador especially in anime circles. He runs a company called Culture Japan and uses the Internet, TV and personal appearances at conventions (as well as secretly dancing around the world dressed as a Star Wars Stromtrooper on youtube videos) to teach people about Japan. His constant companion in this endeavor is his mascot character, Mirai Suenaga. I'm no otaku (anime geek), but I do love visual style and have developed an affinity for the character. She features heavily online and on Japanese language teaching products such as Moekana, a card game for learning Japan's hiragana writing system.

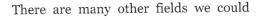

*Danny Choo shows of some of his company's goodies at a convention. The character featured is Mirai, his mascot. Photo appears courtesy of Danny Choo and Mirai Inc.*

Cosplay is another Japan export that has gained huge popularity abroad. Fans make costumes of their favourite anime and game characters, and then they take photographs and attend conventions and competitions. Nowadays, you cannot frequent cosplay circles without hearing the name Alodia Gosiengfiao, though you will have no idea how to spell it, and I bet you have no idea how to pronounce it by reading, but she is also simply known as Alodia, or "the queen of cosplay". She makes the most fantastic costumes herself and with stunning natural, almost ethereal beauty that lends itself well to the elfish characters she often portrays, Alodia smashed her way onto the cosplay scene and quickly rose to her prominent position. She is the biggest celebrity in an ever increasingly popular Japanese export, co-hosting ABS-CBN's *Laugh Out Loud* TV show. She is also an Ani-mate Asia-Animax ambassador and is more recently breaking into the J-pop music scene with her own idol group. She is from the Phillipines.

*Alodia cosplaying as Marvel's Black Widow © Vernieman on Flickr*

There are many other fields we could

discuss but time and space is short (it's also wibbly wobbly, timey wimey). My point is that interest in Japan has spread worldwide, but when you look at books that address Japanese culture a huge majority of them are written not by Japanese, but by foreigners. Did you know that 'foreigner' has the same connotation as 'outsider' over here? Sure the authors may have lived in Japan for many years, but I'm sure they would also be the first to tell you that they are still outsiders. Japanese culture never fully accepts foreigners as native people and even if they did, the mindset of a foreign person is different. They didn't grow up in Japan.

So, how can you expect to get an accurate impression of Japanese culture from a permanent outsider? Never fear, Mukaiyama high school to the rescue!

This articles in this book are written by the Japanese high school students I work with every day. They wrote every word and they chose their own topics. So what you will read about here is what really matters to Japanese teenagers today.

## About the Project's Beginnings

When I first thought of this project there were many things I wanted to do. I wanted to make my mark as an ALT (a position and identity that is soon forgotten by both Japanese teachers and students). I realized I could do this by using my unique skills to do something special. When I thought of what these skills could be the only thing useful that sprung to mind was that I was a writer (with two published books available on Amazon - hint, hint) and I knew how to self-publish a book.

I also wanted to do something exciting that the students would never forget. Most of their lessons are boring, just rote learning and repetition. So, they deserve to have some fun, because they are fun, people; young and exciting with all their own thoughts and emotions that they want to express, but society won't let them.

The other thing that instantly came to mind was that if we published a book it would be available for sale, and that meant money. When I thought about what we could do with money the obvious thing that came to mind was to help local disaster victims. Many people don't know but after the earthquake, tsunami and subsequent nuclear disaster of March 11th, 2011, many people were made homeless, some within a few kilometers of our school, and they are still homeless now. They survived in school halls for up to 6 months and then moved into temporary housing slowly supplied by the government. However, these houses are flimsy and weak, while Japanese weather is harsh to say the least. That was when the project really came together. Not only would students be excited to make a book, but many of them would be ecstatic about helping their local community recover from the disaster. How did I know this? Because they all wrote reports about it the year before.

So, *Let's Pop Culture o(^o^)o* was born. I pooled my resources, spoke to the teachers and we were away. It's not been an easy journey, but I think it has already proven worth it. Of course, an added bonus of doing this project is that it might inspire other English teachers to do something equally exciting, and we are only 3 teachers and 200 students. Just imagine what could be achieved if different schools worked together

### **About the Reviews**

Before we dive into the students reviews, a quick note about what you are about to read. The work is unedited. Please do not be put off by their English mistakes. Think about how hard it is to write an article in a foreign language. After all, I created this project to show the students that they could still make great use of even a beginner's level of English. Most of all, please enjoy the articles we present.

Now, you may be think "The students aren't this good at English! The teacher obviously edited it!" To put it simply, no. You'll see there are plenty of mistakes and I'll tell you why I left them. First of all, it gives an honest impression of students' abilities for all to see, because Japan is often criticized for its English ability. Second, imagine you are a student working on this book. Imagine you work hard over a hot summer to write your article and then when it finally appears in the book, the book you are so excited to see and make, it is changed beyond recognition, because someone has corrected all the mistakes. Its yours no longer. How bad would that make you feel? The main point of this project is to raise the students' confidence, not destroy it.

So, Look what they can do! Seriously, look! They are just learning, but with their words and this book, they have drawn interest to their culture and taught many foreigners about it; they have raised money and awareness for earthquake victims; they have challenged the stale ways of the education system; they have created something they can be proud of for their whole lives. With that confidence, I hope they will try even harder for the future.

Then imagine what they can achieve....

       - Matthew Rowe,
       Mukaiyama H.S. ALT, 2010 - 2013

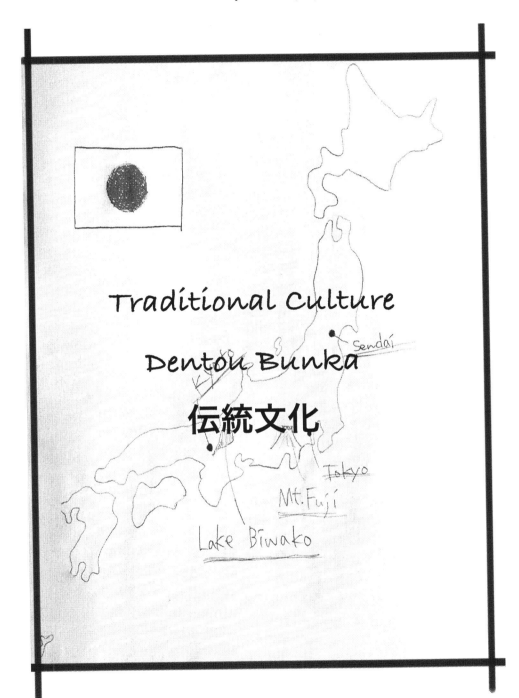

Traditional Culture

Dentou Bunka

伝統文化

## Japanese Language

Japanese is not so much spoken in the world, but of course it is spoken in Japan. Recently, Japanese is popular among foreigners. I think foreigners want to watch Japanese Animation.

There are three types of characters; Hiragana, Katakana and Kanji in Japanese. Hiragana and Katakana are learned when we are elementary school students. Kanji has been learned in elementary school, too, but there are a lot of things I don't know still. There are 48 types of Hiragana and Katakana. On the other hand, there are more than 10,000 different Kanji.

When I was an elementary school student, I was thinking that Kanji is not necessary because there are Hiragana and Katakana. I'm thinking now that we need Kanji because it is hard to read, hard to convey emotion in sentences written only with Hiragana and Katakana. There are different meanings to the same word. For example, there is the word which is said "Kane". This means "a bell" and "cash". Other examples are "Kin", "Kami" etc. "Kin" means "gold", "a fungus", etc. "Kami" means "a god", "paper", "hair", etc. If these are written in only Hiragana or Katakana, people who see these words become confusion.

I hope you read this, if you are interested in Japanese.

## Calligraphy

Calligraphy is a Japanese treasure. Do you know calligraphy? Calligraphy means the art of producing beautiful writing using special pens or brushes, or the writing produced this way. It is one of the parts of traditional culture in Japan. But originally it was introduced from China.

Well, what is the difference between China and Japan about calligraphy? I think it is a difference of kanji or hiragana. China usually writes kanji only, but Japan usually is written hiragana and kanji. So, Japanese looks softer than Chinese. I have studied calligraphy since I was nine years old, and I'm proud of it. Calligraphy is Japanese treasure. But such parts of Japanese traditional culture as this is being forgotten in the present. So, we must spread Japanese culture all over the world.

## Tanka Poems

A 31-syllable Japanese poem. Tanka means short poems. It is made up of 5 sounds, 7 sounds, 5 sounds, 7 sounds and 7 sounds (35 sounds in total). It has been made since the past.

One hundred Tanka poems are very popular. It is composed by one hundred celebrities. More than half of them are Tankas of love. Of course, both of men and women composed them. Some of them are more passionate than others. It is interesting that they didn't use direct words. They composed about scenery but their feelings of love are hidden in it. It is very difficult to compose a Tanka in only 31 sounds. In the old days, composing Tanka was common knowledge. It was a way of making advances to get people to fall in love.

Nowadays, most of Japanese don't compose Tanka. The time has changed. But Tanka is a superb culture, so we shouldn't lose it. A lot of foreigner are interested in Tanka and compose English Tanka recently.

Our feeling cram in only 31 sounds. Skill and experience needed.

## Manner of the Japanese

The Japanese keep good manners. It is important to spend a daily life well. Because manners of the Japanese have consideration for partners, people around the world will be interested in it.

According to the TV program of India, they are impressed with the manners of the Japanese. For example, Japanese take off shoes at school. And put shoes away on shoe shelves. These actions are natural for Japanese, but, Indians wondered. In other words, Indian think manner of Japanese have consideration.

I think Japanese have a delicate sensibility. But that is why Japanese mind too much. If I don't keep manner, someone must wonder or be displeased. Keeping manner is equal to being a good person. It is natural of the Japanese. So I think manners of Japanese have not only consideration but also weak points.

In Japan, keeping manner is equal to being a person. And manner was kept since a long time ago, is an important tradition.

## Edo Gesture

What kind of impression do you have toward a Japanese? It is said that they are well modest, and the Japanese does not show feelings on the face patiently. In today's "THE EARTHQUAKE" I might show such a character of Japanese. 200years ago, Japan was the Edo era then. I think that the custom of people there causes the present character of Japanese. Therefore I want to introduce "Edo gesture".

| Rule (in Japanese) | Example of its use |
|---|---|
| 肩引き<br><br>[kata-hiki] | When passing in a narrow place, the shoulder of each other is pulled. |
| 傘かしげ<br><br>[kasa-kashige] | An umbrella is learned to the side a partner and opposite to so that a drop may not hang down to a partner, when passing an umbrella. |
| すれ違いのまなざし<br><br>[s u r e t i g a i n o manazashi] | Those who will not know if there are eyes is also great. |
| 逆らい仕草<br><br>[sakaraishigusa]: | You must not say "but". |
| う か つ あ や ま り<br>[ukatsuayamari]: | If your foot is stepped on, you will apologize that it was a lack of attention. |
| こ ぶ し う か し<br>[kobushi ukashi]: | When you sit on a seat by ship, shift for a while for the person who came later. |

| Rule (in Japanese) | Example of its use |
|---|---|
| 打てば響<br><br>[uteba hibiku] | I think about a partner, and act immediately |
| お心肥やし<br><br>[osiniko koyashi]: | Maintain one's heart wealthily. |
| 死んだら御免[<br><br>[shindara gomenn] | You have to keep the promise until you died. |
| 陽に生きる<br><br>[hini ikiru]: | A positive thinking. |
| 時泥棒[<br><br>[tokidorobou]: | It being a crime to take the time of the partner. |
| もったい大事[<br><br>[mottai daizi] | It is "mottainai" **Mottainai**: sacrilegious, terribly wasteful |

Those who can not do this action those days were made a fool of, and were targeted by the pick pocket. This action was big required in order that population might pass without a trouble by the Edo which surpasses 1 million people.

Edo behavior is not become a sentence. It is because people were considered to think only feel knowledge when written to the book. Many Edo behavior will be seen even in present Japan, since it is oral culture. And the soul which thinks of a partner is in inherited by the present Japanese.

## A Saying

I want to introduce it because it is deeply connected with everyone's life.

First: "Treasure every encounter, for it will never recur." It means you never know when you meet someone if it will be the last time you'll ever see that person. If it says in Japanese "一期一会." The means same with English.

Second "Every failure is a stepping stone to success." If it says in Japanese "失敗は成功のもと". That means Failure is base of success.

Third: "It is dark at the foot of a candle." In Japanese "灯台もと暗し". 灯台 means a lighthouse. So it means people often know little of what is happening in their own backyards .

There is a saying all over the world, so it has many meanings. I think it is interesting to compare it. I think saying teach to us the wisdom of a life and teachings. My favorite sayings is "It is dark at the foot of a candle" because it is felt familiar.

## Yokai

"Yokai" is Japanese monsters. There is no Japanese person who doesn't know "Yokai." They are imaginary living things. However, Japanese children are familiar with them in the children's stories.

It is because Japanese culture can't be told without them! "Yokai"

appear in Japanese novels, comics, games, movies, anime, as well.

Yokai is a thing of the strong and unusual phenomenon which is beyond an understanding of man in Japan, or the unusual existence with a mysterious power which startles them. It is also called "Ayakashi" or "Mononoke", and "Mamono." Among Yokai, have is the kappa who lives in a river and has a plate in the head, and Tengu which lives in woods and has a long nose. By the way, I like kappa and Nekomata. Nekomata is a cat which has two tails and they often bewitch humans.

It is indispensable to get to know Yokai, if you would like to know Japan well! Because, they appear well in literary works of Japan. For example, representation of Japanese anime "GHIBLI." Many characters which were probably built by reference to Yokai appear in "Spirited Away" and "Princess Mononoke." So are also Japanese-made comics and games. That is, in order to enjoy comics, a novel and a game, a movie of Japanese more, knowledge of Yokai is required!

There are hundreds of Yokai. Although it is scary with Yokai, in order areas, they are worshipped as Gods. Yokai is a pretty deep subject. Yokai each have a unique personality and it is very attractive. Therefore, I want to not only a Japanese but also a foreigner to know about Yokai.

Yokai are unique Japanese monster. They cause fear and have charms.

## Sengoku Busyou (Japanese local military leaders)

The history of loving woman, the game of the Age of Civil Wars, etc attract attention in Japan in recent years. It is because there was an attractive Warring States general, They are called "Sengoku Busyou" or "Sengoku Daimyou.

The persons called "Sengoku Daimyou" were fighting in Japan around the 16th century, aiming at world unification. Especially

Nobunaga Oda, Hideyosi Toyotomi, and Ieyasu Tokugawa are famous. It is not an overstatement although the appearance of three persons finished the Age of Civil Wars.

Although I respect the three people who were introduced in the point, I also want you to know that there is one more person and a wonderful general. The person's name is called Kanetugu Naoe . He was being covered with the helemet of the character of love in the battlefield. And it fought rather than profit for justice.

Although a Warring States general has me, respectively, they suppress Japan and merely think that they wanted to protect people's life. I think that they teach us it is important to have pride.

Local military Leaders (Sengoku Busyou) had strong charisma ,so that they also influenced the present-day Japanese.

## Wasan (Japanese Mathmatics)

About 400 years ago, Japanese people were enjoying mathematics as a hobby. Japan in those days was a closed country, so the Japanese original mathematics developed without being influenced from the Western one. It is called "Wasan" now. Unlike Western mathematics, Wasan was not practical, and was an extention of the people's hobby.

Now, I will present the problem of the famous Wasan. There are many cranes and tortoises. They have 12 heads and 30 legs. How many are there cranes and tortoises repectively? This is called "Tsuru Kame Zan" in Japanese. This problem can be easily solved with simultaneous equations. I set the number of the cranes x, and the number of the tortoises y. Then the following equation makes meet.

$x+y=12$, $2x+4y=30$     When I unite this, $x=9$, $y=3$.

So the cranes are 9, the tortoises are 3.

This problem can be solved even by the elementary school students if they devise. Wasan is almost the easiest problem because it was made as a hobby. But , there are the problems that aren't able to be solved even as the adult.

## The Scenery of Japan

As you know, Japan is the country blessed with rich nature. It is globally known, so people in the world are interested in the beautiful scenery of Japan.

However, naturally what is in Japan is not only rich nature. More than 100 million people live in Japan. As such, in Japan, there are many cities. There are many structures produced by man.

*Sendai, taken from the castle site*

Unlike the historic European cities with building that are aligned with same color and form, Japanese cities seem to be chaotic. There is a unique fun in a Japanese town. When Japan achieved economic growth rapidly, new buildings were elected one after another. They didn't consider the scenery of the town deeply. However, it was also expression of the vitality of the Japanese for recovering from devastation of war.

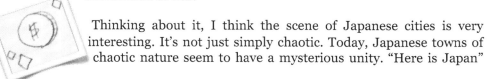

Thinking about it, I think the scene of Japanese cities is very interesting. It's not just simply chaotic. Today, Japanese towns of chaotic nature seem to have a mysterious unity. "Here is Japan"

That consciousness may be making it so.

## The Four Seasons of Japan (1 of 2)

One of the main periods into which a year is divided, each of which has a particular type of weather. There are four seasons of spring, summer, autumn and winter in Japan. Moreover, it is feature of Japan that there are four seasons.

The four seasons are popular among a foreigners. It is because there is special way to enjoy oneself in each of the four seasons. Seeing , listening, and feeling are some of the ways to enjoy them.

There are many features of the four seasons. Trees and a plants bring about change of the four seasons. The cherry trees of pink in full bloom comes in spring. Trees grow luxuriantly in summer. A leaf changes from the green to red or yellow in autumn. A leaf withers in winter and it becomes a preparation period for spring.

Japanese people enjoy a season. People see the cherry blossoms and feel solar warmth in spring. They go to swim in the sea or a pool because summer is very hot. They can see fireworks in summer. In autumn, food is delicious. Some famous foods are a Pacific soury, a chestnut, a matsutake (NB. a type of mushroom), etc. In winter , it is cold and it snows. They stay at home in many cases because it is very cold outside.

You should come to Japan, in order to confirm then.

We have to thank the heat and cold of a natural phenomenon because natural is made by heat and cold. Because the human being has heat and cold, resistance is made and they can live with health for a long time.

I think that as for the four seasons, it is tasteful and is thoughtful. Periods that divide Japanese beauty into four.

## Japanese Four Seasons (2 of 2)

Spring is written in Japanese as "Haru". Summer is "Natsu" in Japanese. autumn is "Aki" in Japanese. Winter is "Huyu" in Japanese.

Japan has four season which have a unique feature. Spring is a warm climate. It is very comfortable for us to pass everyday life, but a few people are suffering from pollen. It causes a sneeze. I am one of the patients. Summer is a warm climate. We are covered in sweat even by stunding. But, when it is a hot day, bathing in the sea makes us happy. Next is autum. In Japanese autum, it is called autum of sports, reading, eating, and art. The school festival is held this season. The last season is winter. Winter is very busy. Because christmas and New Year come in this season. In New Year, all children expect ""Otoshidama". It is small money. So Japanese children become rich in January.

When does it last this beautiful season? The whole world has a serious problem. It is global warning. We depend on the technology. It is very conveniente. But, if this situation lasts, the environmental pollution worsens. We must save this beautifuru season. It is necesarry for us to using machines in our consiousness.

Japanese has particular four season. They makes us happy. We must save this forever.

## Aizuwakamatu is a Japanese town.

It has a very beautiful view and many scence of nature. This town is in Fukushima prefecture. Why is Aizuwakamatu popular? Because Aizuwakamatu has deep history! So Aizuwakamatu became popular, a part of sightseeing, And I love Aizuwakamatu too! I want to live in this town.

Aizuwakamatu has many famous things. For example Akabeko (red cow), Okiagarikoboshi (wobbling toy), Kitakataramen (Chinese noodle soup).

Akabeko is an ornament. I think it looks like a cow. Moreover it's so cute! If you push on the Akabeko's head, Akabeko's neck shakes vertical. Specially I advise you on another; Kitakataramen. It is a noodle, but it isn't ordinary noodles. It's feeling is quite a hard. Japanese people said it has"Nodogosi". Nodogoshi is the feeling of foods going down your throat. It's much better than not having Nodogoshi noodles. Kitakataramen's Nodogoshi is loved by many people. And me too.

*Photo courtesy of Google Maps*

Another, Aizuwakamatu has a castle. It is called"Wakamatujyou"and"Turugazyou". This castle was started in 1384. Wakamatujyo's character "Oshirobokun" was born recently. Oshirobokun looks like a castle and a robot. I think Oshirobokun will be as popular as Akabeko and Kitakataramen

When I went to Aizuwakamatu for the first time, I was an elementary school student. Then I felt delicious Aizuwakamatu's air, because I live in the countryside, and my hometown's air is delicious too. I can't say a good explanation, but if you will come to my hometown or Aizuwakamatu, you can feel the delicious air.

And I like Aizuwakamatu's history. So I will teach you about Aizuwakamatu's history now. First, do you know "Byakkotai"? Byakkotai is a party for the Aizuwakamatu's war. In 1868, but the nominative case party fell down one after another. So Byakkotai had to help for Aizuwakamatu. There the average age is seventeen. They were young people. Japanese man had to go to the war even if they were young. And then Byakkotai's young souls were lost because Aizu of war. I think that things are too awful really I have no feeling for a war continuing now. And I don't want to here a war in the future.

Aizuwakamtu has many culuture things!!

## The Hot Spring (1 of 2)

Hot spring can be by volcano's heat. Natural heat can make it. We can't make it. It is very good for the health when we enter the hot spring. The effect is to heal a stiff neck and be good for skin etc.

In Japan , we has many volcano. So, we have many hot springs. Hakone hot spring, Yuhuin hot spring and Kusatu hot spring are very famous and popular.

Open air bath is outside. So, it can see beautiful scenery there in all year round. Adult people say that to enter it and drink sake is very good. We divides men and women to enter it with nakedness. Hot springs can boil eggs. The egg is called "Hot spring of egg". It is like a boiled egg. It is very delicious. I like it to eat in curry and rice.

Please enter Japan's hot spring and eat hot spring of egg.

## The Hot Spring (2 of 2)

Hot spring can be by volcano's heat. Natural hear can make it. We can't make it. It is very good for the health when we enter the hot spring. The effect is to heal a stiff neck and be good for skin etc.

In Japan , we has many volcano. So, we have many hot springs.

Hakone hot spring, Yuhuin hot spring and Kusatu hot spring are very famous and popular.

Open air bath is out side. So, it can see beautiful scenery there in all year round. Adult people say that to enter it and drink sake (Japanese alcohol) is very good. We divides men and women to enter it with nakedness. Hot springs can boil eggs. The egg is called "Hot spring of egg". It is like a boiled egg. It is very delicious. I like it to eat in curry and rice.

Please enter Japan's hot spring and eat hot spring of egg.

Mmm... egg!

## The Star Festival

In Sendai which we live in, the star festival is popular with many people. In the past, many people prayed, for themselves, which on August 7th. Japan has a lot of traditional stories. "The Star Festival" is one of them. In the past, Vega who is a smart girl and Altair who is a hard worker live in the night sky. And they

Star festival lantern with streamers

married. But they didn't work after they married because they enjoyed their life too much. So, God pulled apart them. And they couldn't meet each other expect July 7th. Now, the calendar is different the old ways. So, we hold the festival in August 7th.

Thousands of people visit the star festival every year from many places. The best point is the big decorations which says "Fukinagashi"(streamers). These decollate the shopping district

and the station. They look very beautiful because they have many colors. Many people enjoy wearing "Yukata" and "Uchiwa" (type of fan) that is the traditional things.

I love the Star Festival because I have been to the festival since I was a child. And also, we can eat delicious foods at many street stalls. So we can enjoy looking and eating. Would you come to Sendai on August 7th?

It's a Japanese traditional festival. It makes Sendai and people vigorous.

## Hina Doll Set

From the China. Start date is before about 1,000 years. "Hina doll set"is used on March 3. It is the day to pray for healthy growth and happiness for young girls. It is also called "Momo no sekku" or Peach festival. Most families with girls display dolls called Hina-ninngyo. It was believed that the dolls protected people from sickness or ill-fortune.

A long time ago, people threw paper dolls into rivers and in the sea to drive away. Little girls wear special clothes "Kimono". It is very beautiful. People began displaying dolls in the Edo period. The dolls display going. People are dressed in beautiful ancient court costumes. Today, we eat traditionally disher like Chirashizushi and clam soup for the name for the doll festival.

"Hina doll set"is girls day. Hina-ninngyo is very cute, and girls is very cute. March 3 is special day for little girls. It made their happy.

29

## New Year's Eve Bells

We strike a bell 108 times at the temple on New Year's Eve to get rid of our 108 spiritual darkness and greet the New Year with an innocent heart. While we listen to the sound of the bell, we reflect on our behavior in the year.

"108" generally means the number of human spiritual darkness of 108 times, we strike a bell 107 times in the last year, we strike a bell once in the New Year. We can strike a bell for free in many temples. We watch people striking a bell on a TV program called "the old year and the new year". The sounds of a bell which others strike enable us to get rid of our spiritual darkness. That is why everyone can help each other. It was originally, that we struck a bell at the end of the year to greet a god with an innocent heart.

I listen to the sound of the bell every year with my family. While we eat buck wheat noodles eaten on New Year's Eve. I become composed when I listen to that sound. I really think that my spiritual darkness have been cleared away. There are some temples which can't have a striking a bell because of complaints but I think that striking a bell is a good custom. We should keep this custom. That is why I want to strike a bell at lease once in my life.

We strike a bell 108 times in the last day of year before and after midnight to get rid of our 108 spiritual darkness and greet the New Year. I think it's a good custom in Japan.

## Fireworks

Fireworks are very beautiful . And it delights the eyes of the watcher to see fireworks. So the fireworks are popular with both children and adults.

The fireworks mainly can be watched in Summer. In a fireworks display, we can watch very large fireworks. There are sparklers which can be done in various places. The fireworks can create a festive atmosphere. And it has various colors such as red, blue, yellow and  green. The fireworks such as heart and ribbon are very cute.

I think fireworks can make people smile. Fireworks is very beautiful. I often did a sparkler with my sibling, my cousin and my grandfather. I have liked the fireworks since then. We can buy reasonable the firework. And we can enjoy. It is very fun for me to do a sparkler with my friend.

Firework bring us the real feeling of summer.

## Kimono

Clothes ordinary Japanese with a kimono. In recent years, it is considered also as the folk costume in Japan. It is also called Japanese clothes and dry goods.

*Mako girls in Kyoto, wearing kimono*

A kimono makes long arrival fix to the body by tying a belt with the position of the waist. It has a sleeve much larger than the thickness of an arm. In long arrival or a haori (NB. long sleeved coat), the past is sewn among sleeves and, thereby, a cuff becomes shorter than sleeve length. And, a bodily outline game appears only in the shoulder and the waist,    and,    as for other portions,    the object for males and the object for women are covered almost superficially with a kimono. So, when we wear kimono, not only we can relax, but also we are looked beautiful.

Kimono is thought it is old and not good. But I don't think so. In certain, many people usually don't wear kimono. But I think that kimono is good to wear at the time of the ceremony of the fine turning point of life. For example, Shichigosan, coming-of-age ceremony, and a graduation ceremony. Also there are many people who wear a kimono then.

It seems show that kimono is still very good for Japanese. If a kimono isn't wearied many times by many people, it is liked by many Japanese.

## Yukata (1 of 3)

Yukata is Japanese costume summer. Every summer, most of people wear. It is very beautiful. Yukata was everyday clothes in the past. Kimono is very popular such as Japanese costume in the world. Yukata is light and cool more than Kimono. So, people wear in summer. Yukata made one long cloth that is Tanmono (NB. Fabric). And it ties by Obi that long and hard cloth. Tie's way of Obi is many ways.

*Yukata courtesy of Kenichi Nobusue on Flickr*

I like Yukata. Because, that beautiful old tradition's pattern. I like very much it. I think that I wear it every summer.

Yukata is Japanese costume that has beautiful old tradition's pattern.

## Yukata (2 of 3)

Yukata is airy and easy to wash. Besides, with a low price too, it is easy to look right in this dress.

Yukata is a kind of Kimono and it is made from cotton. It was popular in the Edo period. It was called "yukatabira" from the first one (NB. ). After a long time "yukatabira" changed to "yukata". People get a Yukata only in summer time, almost every day, but Kimono sometimes.

To get "yukata" is a good idea to spend a very hot summer comfortably in Japan. We want to continue this good Japanese custom. Many summer festivals in Tohoku have many chances to get "yukata" now a days. I want to tell of this custom in the future.

# Yukata (3 of 3)

"Yukata" is very airy because it's made of hemp. And to wear Yukata is easer than Kimono, so it's worm by many Japanese. Especially, Yukata is loved by many Japanese girls because it's very cute. It has various color and designs.

It's a kind of Japanese summer dress. It's used by many Japanese people since about the Heian era. It has many advantages. First, it's very airy. When we wear it we fell cool. Second, it's cheaper than Kimono. Moreover to wear it is very easy. So we can easily experience the Japanese cultures. Etc...

I feel in love with it when I was a little child because Yukata is very cute. When I go to a fireworks display and a summer festival, I go there in Yukata. It is a pity we cannot wear it all seasons. We can wear it in summer only.

It's Japanese dress for summer. It is loved by many Japanese and very popular. When we wear it, we can experience the Japanese cultures. The charms are very airy and cheaper than Kimono and cute. I like it, too, very much! And I want to wear it next summer too.

# Sensu (Folding Fan)

It is sent when a friends has a ceremonial occasion because it well. It was made in Japan in 973. Uchiwa was made before that. It is very popular in foreign countries.

What is it used for; When you laugh, the mouth is hidden by it. The new years day, you send to your eternal friend. In rakugo (NB. see later), a comic storyteller use instead of chopsticks. It is very useful and very compact. Sensu differs from Uchiwa (NB. plain fan) mainly because of its compact shape when folded, making it easier than to carry.

Sensu is very compact. And how many designs on the fans surface.

If you want, you can make your original Sensu so you will want to use it more. It is simple and useful, I think it is real high performance thing. My sensu's design is Woodstock (NB. from 'Peanuts' comic strip). Very very Cuuute!!! I think it is good to collaborate Japanese culture and foreign culture.

I do love it, Sensu! This is very useful, and very cool. I expect your 'sensu' (sense).

## Furoshiki (Japanese cloth)

The origin, thirteen century, who is not clear, but Japanese made it. Furoshiki is a square a cloth. It can wrap various things. For example, clothes, bottles, books, and so on. It also can become a bag.

It become the center of public attention recently because we can use it instead of vinyl bag. It dates back to the thirteen century. When we go to a public bath, it wraps our clothes. After our bath we used it to dry ourselves. We don't use it in the bathroom at present, but it is active in the different scenes. It can wrap a water melon, some plastic bottles, some text books ,etc. Besides it can be worn as a cap to protect against the heat, it can cover our legs like a blanket.

I think that it is very useful because it can transform into a lot of forms. I think it has strong points. For example it is light and it isn't bulky. It is eco friendly because it can be used any member of times. Therefore it has been loved by Japanese for many years, but I think it has weak points.

For instance, if it can't wrap tightly, something falls from it. It also has an old fashioned. I don't use it, but my grandmother had used by two years ago. It's an all around cloth. It makes our life convenient.

# Fuurin (a wind bell)

A wind bell has been loved by Japanese since Edo era. It is made of glass shaped in a wooden bowl with a short of iron and an ornament of a paper. The sound makes us cool when the hot day is here.

We Japanese, we don't know why, when we hear the sound, we could think of a brook. So we can feel cool. The truth is the sensible temperature fell. But there are effects only to Japanese. I saw on the TV, foreigners who don't know about the wind bell hearing the sound in an experimentation. Just then, their sensible temperature rose in an instant. Because they began to be angry when they felt the sound was noisy.

I like this wind bell. Because it makes use of what is a sensible only Japanese. I was surprised to hear that foreign people don't recall a brook when they hear the sound. That means that Japanese are sensitive and gifted and there are many natural things near to us. I think that if the wind bell is not in Japan, it is meaningless. It existing in Japan, Japanese 's sensitive to our bringing up.

A wind bell is used in the summer. A breath of air is made the sound. The sound makes Japanese cool. A wind bell is tasteful to only Japanese.

# Tatami (straw mats)

Tatami is made by Japanese people in the Heian period. Tatami is Japanese culture and evidence that old Japanese people lived. It's popular because it's Japanese tradition. Also its fragrance is good! Tatami fragrance   of forest. I like it.

Tatami is made straw and a tatami border. Its shape is rectangle and it is 180 centimeters wide and 90 centimeters long. It's about five centimeters thick. Also there are Japanese house. We can get at the shopping mall or tatamiya (NB. Tatami shop). It's very high price. But it can't do anything one piece.

Tatami breathes well, so it useful in summer. But it absorbs moisture, so not clean. So we have to change regularly. In short, tatami is high price.

Tatami is very popular because it is Japanese tradition. My house has it. I like smell of it. It makes my feeling good. I wish that tatami is loved by people of the whole world.

## Shogi (Chinese chess)

*A shoji board courtesy of Matt Pereault on Flickr*

It was introduced to Japan from China in the Heian era. Today, it has spread among many people as an "interesting board game" because it is very easy and strategic. Oda and Tokugawa and Hideyoshi who is the famous historical person played Shogi old years ago.

The board is almost made of woods. It's value is a broad range, cheep and expensive. Twenty pieces are your friends. Hisha(like rook), Kaku(like bishop), Keima(like Knight), Kyosha(chess has not it that like Kyosha),Hu(like a pown), and Ou(like King). When you beat your opponent's king, you win the game.

Many thrilling tactics is good point in Shogi. Possibly experienced people of chess think that we do not have to playing Shogi But , "Shogi" has many specific rules and great tactics that chess does not have. The rule always you to spend one turn to put a piece you free space on the board (needless to say, don't pile up on your piece) In short, it is maybe that opponent's Queen looms next to your king. Thanks to this rule, you make a camp or castle, offence or defense, both them, you are free to choose. Japanese tend to prefer defense. Me too! Especially, I like defensive tactics said "A bear's den". It is contents that you put a king at the corner and are encircled with about a dozen pieces."Stand Hisha(like rook) " is very offensive tactics. Moreover, "Stand Hisha and A bear's den" is a hybrid tactics. It is very fantasy that offense plus defense equal very strong defense!

## Shamisen (Japanese guitar)

I will introduce about a Shamisen. It is created 500 years ago. Shamisen is a famous of a tradition Japanese musical instrument. It is popular with elderly people.

Shamisen is a music instrument. It is made of wood and animal skin. There are many kinds of Shamisen. Its sound is very nice but it is difficult to play the Shamisen. People play the Shamisen with other traditional Japanese musical instrument.

I hope that Shamisen will be popular with young people. Young people do not know much of Shamisen. I think Shamisen is great music instrument. So I hope that know more about Shamisen.

I want more people to know the Shamisen.

## Electone

It is an interesting musical instrument. It's like a keyboard. We can do an easy ensemble by using it.

Electone was completed in 1958 as a trial product. The next year, it began selling in Japan. Electone has U.K.(upper keyboard), L.K. (lower keyboard), p keyboard, expresson pedal and second expresson pedal. Upper keyboard is to play the main melody on your right hand. Lower keyboard is to play chord on your left hand. Pedal keyboard is to play base sound on your left foot. Expresson pedal and second expresson pedal can control big sound or small sound with your right foot.

I think electone's charm point is to make some kinds of tones. We can enjoy the   sound of various musical instrument.  It is difficult to play, because you have to use both hands and both feet.  But, as for me, the joy when music comes to play is unforgettable.  Various functions are usable, they have a floopy disk drive.  You can load new sounds.

Because an electone is a musical instrument able to use the various functions, it is really fun.

## Sadou

It's Japanese traditional way of Tea Ceremony performance. The origin of "sadou" goes back to the middle era; 15th century in Japan. It used to be popular only among the high-society class and feudal warriors (so called "samurai" or "bushi") since then, it has been gradually widely spread to the common people.

Japanese people like their green tea itself, and the "sadou" does not require any particular, huge equipment.

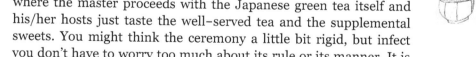

"Sadou" is the special Japanese traditional way of Tea Ceremony where the master proceeds with the Japanese green tea itself and his/her hosts just taste the well-served tea and the supplemental sweets. You might think the ceremony a little bit rigid, but infect you don't have to worry too much about its rule or its manner. It is true that the "sadou", as the Japanese art requires certain style of manners and rules of the activites. Since tea-making activity should be seemed to be beautiful and elegant for the host and the others, but, you as the guest of the ceremony, can taste it as you like. Through the Japanese Tea Ceremony, I think you can certainly have a chance to understand the Japanese unique way of thinking as well.

Under the manner of the "sadou", hosts are usually quite recommended that they shall avoid the front face of things. For example, the host will be required to avoid the front face of the Tea-bowl when they just started drinking the tea. So the host will rotate the bowl a little bit in order not to use the front face of the bowl but to use the bowl indirectly.

This "indirection" oriented way of thinking is the very key point of "sadou". This "indirection" way of manner seems to be regard as the Japanese virtue. The typical Japanese people prefer the "indirect" way of expression to a direct one. Moreover Japanese people will often guess what the other people really want to say Because common Japanese people will not often use the straight forward expression. "Read the between the lines" becomes to be quite natural among the Japanese people.

I think the indirect and moderate manner is thought to be good to show our respect to others or to important things such as tea ceremony tools which belongs to the master of tea ceremony.

In this way, the "sadou" is not just only tea party itself, but the Japanese culture itself. The "sadou" seems to be the typical type of Japanese traditional human behavior, and the Japanese culture itself and even their philosophy.

Why not try this good taste of the Japanese green tea and their culture? Once you have it, you can never miss it again. I'm quite sure of this.

## Rakugo: "Manjyu Kowai" ("Japanese sweets are scary")

Comic storytelling in Japanese is rakugo. Rakugo is part of Japanese funny story, variety show there is a funny ending. Rakugo has all kinds of stories. This time I'll introduce the story of "manjyu kowai". This story outline is, several young people with free time gathered, each had a scary thing they disliked. Everybody said "spider", "snake", "ants", and only one person was miserable and afraid of what crap he craved is one scary mystery to the others.

"I had none. "said the man.

They press him just in case, and "there is really no scary thing?" they asked.

"It is nothing!" he says.

However, on pushing the case several times reructantly confesses with " the truth." When asking what he hates he says: "manjyu scary." The man became sick by manjyu talk only "and" says, "I'll fall asleep in the next room." So everyone urged him.

"He is dissatisfied by the manjyu , finds it offensive , threatening to him."

So they bought a lot of manjyu , dumped it in the next room . Then the scared man woke up.

"Oh scary, scary. Let's go without the wait, to eat is such a scary thing. Too good lot, a taste is scary." And says him eating manjyu, munching, and finally he ate the whole.

Thank you, it's appearance is amusing. They watched the progression in the snake peek and are noticed by me. Everyone got angry

"What's your real scary stuff!"

"The most of scary thing is dark tea."

This story's seasoning is the man cheated other men into getting manjyu , and what's more, he requested dark tea. I think it is funny story, and this story is teached Japanese language interest by us.

I'm happy if you are interested in rakugo I propose to study about rakugo.

## Sushi

I will introduce sushi. Sushi is the soul food of Japan. Sushi is a food that has raw fish placed on the small size rice. Sushi was born in the Edo period. Sushi is very expensive but we can eat it low cost in

Sushi courtesy of Ulterior Epicure on Flickr

"kaitennsushi"(NB. Conveyer belt sushi). Kaitennsushi is very strange shop. All sushi is riding on rails and turning inside the shop. I have ever eaten, such as tuna, salmon, shrimp, squid and scallops.

Sushi has a lot of kinds. For example, chirashisushi, inarisushi, makisushi, and nigirisushi.(NB. Sushi in a box with sprinkled ingredients, sushi wrapped in fried tofu, sushi rolls and plain sushi respectively) Nigirisushi is the most of popular.

I think sushi is an invaluable food for Japanese.

## Soba

"Soba" is very popular in Japan. It is a kind of noodle. "Soba" has many types that can be divided into cold ones and hot ones. So we can enjoy it all the year and it is one of the reason why it is popular.

Details are unclear, history of "Soba" is very old. "Soba" is my favorite food and everyone may love it. It tastes very nice. What is more, it is cheap and easy to get.

It is difficult to explain "Soba". It has many types and each of it has original taste, and it'll be a joy of eating them. "Soba" is easy to cook, so you can make your own original "Soba". It has infinity potential.

"Soba" is a kind of noodle. It has many ways to arrange and potential is infinity! Let's try it!

# Raw egg rice

Raw egg rice is a very popular Japanese food. A raw egg put on the rice. We shake the rice and raw egg. But, not every Japanese like it.

A raw egg is put on the rice, and shaking it. At last, soy source pour in a proper amount is put on it. Then eat it. It tastes a little salty and a little sweet.

Putting a fresh raw egg on the rice is very delicious. But, not fresh is no good. It can not eat at the school. It can make me. Making it is very easy. Children can make it. Very delicious and makes me happy. Raw egg rice is the most  famous of Japanese food in the world.

# Umeboshi (Pickled Plum)

Do you know "Umeboshi"? It is food. Maybe all Japanese people know it.  It is a pickled plum and sour. You can eat it with Onigiri (rice ball).  It is red, too sour for me to eat.. Do you think that you want to eat? You should eat it with rice once.

Someone may call us, Japanese people "Umeboshi man" If I am called that, I don't get angry. Let's go to Japan! I'll show you.

I often wrote lies. Please don't worry! You can know "Umeboshi" if you go to Japan. I am looking forward to seeing you. See you!

## Hinomaru-Bento

"Hinomaru" means the Japanese flag.
"Bento" means a box lunch in Japanese. It is
made from rice and umeboshi. Umeboshi is
pickles of a plum, a Japanese apricot. It looks
like the Japanese flag. We can make it cheap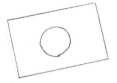
because we only use rice and umeboshi. Umeboshi preserves the
rice. It stops it from spoiling. Sometimes, it appears in the movie
which is set in the Showa-Era.

I think Hinomaru-Bento is the most economical box lunch, and
umeboshi and rice, that is, red and white is auspicious for Japan.
But I think no one bring it to school now. We don't feel full if we eat
it.

Hinomaru-Bento is auspicious and everyone knows it.

## Japanese food "Mochi"

Mochi is the rice cake. It is known as a Japanese food, but we use it
an other way. I want to tell you the "other way." Mochi is used as a
present when we have congratulatory events. We put two mochis
which are a red one and a white one in the box.

There are a lot of foods particular to Japan. For example, Sushi,
Tempra (deep fried shrimp), Sukiyaki (beef slices friend with
vegetables) Miso soup, and mochi. This time I want to explain
Mochi — it is a rice cake — because Sushi, Tempra, ... are popular,
so you already know them. There are many kinds of mochi like
kashiwa-mochi, kusa-mochi, kagami-mochi, and sakura-mochi.

Japanese people bring mochi whenever we have congratulatory
events. For example, the New year, wedding, entrance ceremony,
graduation ceremony and when we build a new house. Usually
mochis are prepared in one pair, red and white. There are known as
lucky colors in Japan. Regrettably, I can't find this system lately. I
think that it is one part of Japanese culture, so we had better keep

continuing it for the future.

Mochi is recognized as not only food, but also a greeting thing. I introduced when it is used as a greeting thing in Japan.

## Beni Imo Taruto (Red Potato Tarts)

It is a cake called the rouge potato tart which production of the cake called porsceh of the okashi, a company selling made that I introduced. It is one of the most popular souvenirs in Okinawa.

There are three characteristics of the deep red potato. The parple that the first is colorful. Because the raw materials are deep red potatoes of the Okinawa product. Second, there have the rich flaver and sweetness of the deep red potato. The third does not use the food additives such as preservatives. So it is mild on our body.

## Wagashi (1 of 2)

*Wagashi courtesy of [puamelia] on Flickr*

Wagashi is Japanese sweets. Wagashi is made by craftsman.

Wagashi is a traditional Japanese sweet. They are the sweets eaten before drinking powdered green tea in the tea ceremony and they are congenial with tea. They are healthy.

Wagashi, which is suited for every season of the year, are made. They, which wagashi craftsman made are very beautiful and very delicious. It's art. Wagashi is made from sugar and bean paste. Everyone can buy them in a Wagashi shop.

I disliked wagashi until I belonged to the tea ceremony club but when I belonged to the tea ceremony club and I ate wagashi I thought "It is very delicious." So I can eat wagashi now.

Today, Japanese people seldom eat wagashi. I want many more people to eat wagashi because wagashi is low in calories and good for health. I think people should eat wagashi more than cake.

Wagashi is a traditional Japanese sweet and very delicious.

# Wagashi (2 of 2)

I want to introduce "wagashi". "Wagashi" is a Japanese traditional sweet. It is an old one and was eaten over one thousand years ago, but frits eaten now too.

"Wagashi" can make at home but it is a littie hard. Because Japanese people almost "wagashi" bought in market. but people making sweets well that "wagashi" making in the home. That often uses "azuki" that is Japanese paple beans and it is low in calories.

"Azuki" is boild and suger added that called "annko". "Annko"is paste that called "koshiann" not paste called "tsubuann". There are bought in the Japanese supermarket. "Wagashi" has a lot of value. Not used "annko" and used it. Other "wagashi" is elaborate figure it like a flower. It is very beauty.

I want to introduce "wagashi" , it is called "hagi-no-tsuki". It is a speciality in Miyagi,  that is cake in cream .it is very good. I like

"wagashi" because  I like sweet, I want to a lot of people taste it. I

think "wagashi" is good . but many people maybe do not like it.

# Vending machines

About B.C. 215, they were invented by ancient Egyptians. Vending machines are very convenient. Vending machines of drinks are put around the cities in Japan. So people can buy it quickly when they want something to drink.

Things sold by vending machines are different. For example, snacks, foods, talismans, etc. Capsule toys are also one of them. But not all capsule toys can give what you want because capsule toys give things of its series at random. Therefore people often get the identical toy. Conversely the toys that are hard to get are a rarity. The pleasure of using capsule toys will be to get the rare toys.

Reason of using vending machines is two things. First, they are convenient. Second, they sell rare or funny items. Actually, I almost everyday use them because they are convenient. And it cost my uncle a lot of money to using capsule toys for getting rare or funny items.

Vending machines got to be popular because they give easily us things we want when we need.

## Otaku (Anime geek)

It is suppose that it has a peculiar behavioral
pattern and culture. If people want to be absorbed in comics and anime. It can be easly absorbed as a hobby. It is popular.

The definition what a freak is not established. What is depended on each time and what the word means by a critic is not constant. Commonly, it may be strongly connected to keywords such as a fetish and akihabara  geeks (NB. Akihabara is an area of Tokyo where electronics and anime products are sold in great number). Concerning deeply in a hobby and things in dictionary explained as a person who lacks the other extensive know ledge and sociality.

I like "otaku" because they are animating in Japan. I think that it may be active unless trouble is made for others. It is glad that Japanese culture is admired from the world. Otaku is more famous since 1970.

# School Uniform

I'll explain about school uniform. School uniform is a school symbol. They are cool and cute. There are many kinds. For example, sailor-suit top and pleated shirt, blazer and so on. School uniform is different at each school.

*Photo courtesy of Sano Design on Deviant Art*

School uniforms have a very old history. Japanese students have put on school uniform since the Meiji Era. My friends have a longing for them. Mukaiyama high school doesn't have school uniform. We have plain clothes. I like plain clothes but my friends don't like that. My friends said, "Plain clothes is troublesome, and school uniform is too cute!"

In general, high school students put on school uniform. But it's with no individuality. I think that plain clothes develop one's originality. So I like it. But school uniform is a wonderful part of Japanese culture. If you will come to Japan, please put on school uniform. You may like school uniform!

Thank you!

# Purikura (1 of 3)

The Japanese word "Purikura" is a shortened from of the name "Print Club" of the game centre's photo machine. It's especially popular with young people, because it takes very good picture.

How to use this machine: First, go into a box and take a picture. Next, we do the decoration of this picture with a stamp, a font and writing a pen. The Purikura which was printed fin. On the picture we can write today's news and about a good friend and so on when decorating the picture. It will be something pleasant to look back on. I have many these!

Please drop in by all means when you come to Japan!

## Purikura (2 of 3)

Photo courtesy of Loose Punctuation on Flickr

Purikura's real name is "Print club." This is the machine to take photographs. We can write letters and draw pictures on the photographs. That's why it is popular with Japanese girls.

Purikura machines are amusement arcade. There are many kinds of Purikura. For example, "LADY BY TOKYO", "Viva Jyoshi", "Heroine Face", etc. These are very difficult. Purikura can change our eye size in the photographs. The eyes sizes are different on Purikura models. Our faces in the photographs are different, too. So everyone chooses models they like.

I don't always change my eye size because I think eyes sizes changed are too big. But I enjoy writing letters and drawing pictures on the photographs.

We often say, "Let's take Purikura!" We can make our memories with friends by taking Purikuras. So I think Purikura is popular with Japanese girls. I think Purikura is one of the best tools to make friends.

## Purikura (3 of 3)

First sold in 1995 for 400 yen. This is a machine where we can leave recollections. We can take photographs and a character and stamp can be put into the photograph. Japanese people use this in order to become friendly with people. To write "good friends "on the photograph with the person, we can get friendship. So Purikura has been popular for over ten years.

First we pay 400 yen. Then take photographs. Next, move to "rakugaki (NB scribbling) corner "and scribble on photographs for a few minutes. Last we receive the photograph seal, finished!

We can write words with a lot of color's pens and put stamp in "rakugaki corner". There are many stamp, for example heart, star etc. Also we can change our hair color and wear glasses and a hat. We can select the size and the number of sheets. We can get the photographs in mobile phones.

We take 10 ~ 15 minutes to make Purikura. When we are in a hurry, we can't take Purikura. Its cost is a little expensive for me.

This makes young people a captivated. It makes our eyes so big and makes our skin clear. Our faces get so cute or cool, more than real faces. Taking Purikura is pleasant. Purikura is a machine which contracts the distance between each other.

## Kaomoji: Picture and Language

Japanese kaomoji (NB face characters) is more cuter t h a n foreign once. It is very useful to tell our feeling. For example, when I exchange e-mail. I use those. Now, it become cute goods: *Gotouchi-shobon*. I love it.

(ˆ − ˆ)   (T^T)   (● ˋ 3 ´●)

Would you see those Kaomoji?   Those Kaomoji is Japanese Kaomoji. On the other hands, foreign ones is like this.

:-)      :-(      :-<

Both Japanese one of Foreign ones appear smile, crying, angry. Japanese ones is richer of feeling expression than foreigners. I like this (´ · ω · ˋ). This tells sadly feeling. I use them wanting to tell our feeling. Japanese Kaomozi is wonderful!

# Masking tape

Masking tape is used to decorate something. It has many kinds of patterns. It is made by Japanese washi (paper).

Masking tape is kind of stationery. It is popular with a wide generation. The pattern of the Masking tape is stripe or dot, check, and so on. It is used for many ways. It's very convenience.

I like Masking tape and I have a lot of it. I use it to stick notes, files and so on. It is very useful. So, many people buy it and use it. Because masking tape is made by washi, it is different from other tape.

Because Masking tape is very cute and useful. So it is popular.

# Shibaken

Shibaken is a Japanese dog. It is very lovely, and strong. Since it is easy to keep, it's popular in Japan. Many people keep shibaken.

Shibaken was specified as the natural treasure of Japan in 1936. The features of a shibaken are short hair, the ears which stands, small size, etc. Shibaken is clever and faithful to an owner. Since it's popular, there are movies and books of shibaken in Japan.

I like shibaken too. I think that shibaken is one of the symbols of Japanese culture. Shibaken is loved by Japanese people. Since shibaken is nervous and stubborn, it's unsuitable for small children. However, shibaken is brave and excellent. I'm very glad because shibaken is popular also in foreign countries these days. I want shibaken to become more popular in foreign countries.

Shibaken is a dog representing Japan.

## Kendo

Kendo has a long history. Kendo has its origin in the Heian period. It was in the Edo period that it became the present form.

When I practice Kendo, I wear a padded sleeveless undergarment, hakama and "Bogu". "Bogu" are men, kote and dou. It is such as armour. I use "Shinai"."Shinai" is made of bamboo. I hit men or kote or dou with a "Shinai".

The game is four minutes. The winner is the person who hits men or kote or dou more than the opponent during the four minutes. But Kendo is not a sport. Kendo is a martial art. So only hitting them, I can't win. Spirit and pose is very important. Winning the game is difficult. So, when I win the game, I feel very good!!

This year, the Olympics was held in London. Kendo isn't an Olympic item. Why will there not be Kendo in the Olympics? There are two reasons that I think about. First, this is because it is difficult to judge it. When spirit and attitude after having beaten are not set, it dosen't become "Ippon"(a point). When I hit men or kote dou, it becomes "Ippon". So, "Ippon" is very vague. Second, this is because it avoids becoming a competition. Kendo is not a competition. It dosen't "Ippon" only by having hit it. I think I want to prevent it from becoming a sport where only hits are important.

Kendo is very difficult and very hard. But it is very exciting. Kendo is a martical art. It is the sport that can teach courtesy.

# Kyudo

Kyudo is one of the Budo in Japan. It is like archery. A chance to do Kyudo is very few. Basically , there are only Kyudo clubs in the high schools. The club in the junior high school is rare. So some junior high school students work hard to belong to the club in the high school. As a result, the numbers in the club are many. By the way, my club had sixty people, summing up from freshmen to senior.

You may think Kyudo is only hitting a target with an arrow. When you hear of Kyudo, but in fact, it isn't very simple. First, Kyudo   emphasize spirit more than hitting a target. So it doesn't have a score system, only hitting a target or not hitting. Second, importance of movement. Even if you can hit a target well, if the movement is bad. It is not good. Arranging the movement is Kyudo's essence.

I think Kyudo is very complex. Other sports and Budo don't have it. But it's very interesting. Kyudo is one of the Budo in Japan. It's essence is deep.

# Judo

Judo is a japanese sport. It was invented by Bushi in meiji era.

Judo's history is very long. Judo became part of the Olympic Games in 1994. Judo has been popular to a lot of people because practice makes people very strong. Not only physically but also mental affects are common.

Judo has a lot of waza (technique). For example ashiwaza , nagewaza and so on (leg techniques, throwing techniques) . For instance, kesagatame (mat hold). And Judo is a sports that two means aim to get Ittipon (one point). It is interesting in rapidly changing offence and defence.

Photo courtesy of Bundeswehr Fotos on Flickr

I've never played. Judo , but I like to watch it on TV. Judo is a soul battle. There is a really strong human. In the first place., almost all Japanese sports don't use items. So Japanese sports show us their soul.

Judo is an exciting sport in the world. Because it showed us the men's real soul and beauty.

## Japanese Soccer

Japanese soccer is developing now. Because some Japanese soccer player are activity in the world.

There is J League in Japan. We can get excited every week. But, they don't have to win the foreign soccer club. I think Japanese soccer will develop in future too. I'm sure that many soccer players advance in to foreign. Because "Samurai Japan" and "Nadeshiko Japan" made rapid progress in the London Olympic.

So, I want to notice Japanese soccer.

# J. League

1993 start   soccer league (in Japan) J. League has Divition 1 and Division 2. Division 1 has 18 teams. Division 2 has 22 teams. In total, 40 teams join this league. Japanese soccer fans call Division 1 "J1",and Division 2 "J2". 36 matches take place in the year. 2012 in J1. 44 matches take place in the year 2012 in J2.

There are many famous players who grew up in the J. League. for example, Shinji Kagawa who is active in Manchester United of England, Yuto Nagatomo who is active in Inter of Italy etc. In recent years, players who are active all over the world emerge like Shinji Kagawa and Yuto Nagatomo. There are a lot of promising players in the J. League. so, this league improve little by little.

My favorite team is Vegelta Sendai. This team is my hometown`s team. I have been cheering for this team since I was in elementary school. This teams is growing stronger gradually every year. This team is to aim for the championship position in the J. League this year. I want this team to get the championship, the momentum of this remains to be seen.

There are few representatives of the overseas players in J. League. If representatives of the overseas players come   to   play in Japan,

this league will warm up more than now.

J. League lets us feel excited in each game. Please go to stadiums to see a game once by all means.

# Vegelta Sendai Football Club

Because it is a soccer team in Japan. They are soccer player in Vegelta. They are skillful.

My country has a soccer team. It is Vegelta Sendai. Vegelta joined the J league. J league is Japan's league of soccer. Vegelta is strong in this year. It will be winning in the league this year.

I want people know J league all over the world. J league is very great. Because every team is strong. So we enjoy to cheer for team. I often watch game at the stadium. Then I am exciting.

I want people know J league all over the world.

## The Japanese girl soccer team "Nadesiko Japan"

Nadesiko Japan is Japan's soccer team. Why is the team popular? The answer is that Nadesiko is so strong! 2012 FIFA world cup's champion is this team.

Nadesiko Japan is so strong! The team's captain "Homare Sawa" is good at soccer. Her performance charms all of fan. When in the 2012 world cup, Japan and America fought. It was a good game. Real ability will out in the end. I went to cheer the team. I have cheered it since 3years ago.

This year, at the London Olympic, Nadesiko Japan got a silver medal. I became more of a fan! Nadesiko Japan is very popular. I think that Nadesiko has three good points. 1.So strong

2. Their play is so excellent

3. Their smile is good

So I love NADESIKO JAPAN!

## Nadeshiko's Captain Homare Sawa

The Nadeshiko team became popular because they won the World Cup in 2011. They have been known well by Japanese since then. I have been cheering a woman

Homare Sawa on a vending machine advert

in the team. Her name is Homare Sawa.

She has been done bullying in her childhood (NB. She was bullied). But she has liked to play soccer and, good soccer player since then. She practiced very hard day after day. At last, she entered the World Cup in 2011 as the Nadeshiko team. I think that the team won because of her activity then. And, the team became popular this start. She is 33 old years. But, she is a soccer player on the active list.

I think that it is important for us to be absorbed something. And I think to continue something will have an effect to own future.

Because the Nadeshiko Japan won the World Cup in 2011, they became popular. I think it is wonderful thing.

## Uchimura Kohei

Born in 1989, he is proffesional gymnast player. He got a gold medal in the London Olympic games. First he won a silver medal in the Peking Olympic games when he was nineteen. So he became a famous gymnast player.

He won a silver medal at a group and a floor event. And he won a gold medal at an individual event in London Olympics. He became a hero. His charming point is a perfect landing. Many people can not do a perfect landing But Uchimura player can do a beautiful landing. There are many fans who think it is very cool J.

He was born in 1989 in Fukuoka. He began to be a gymnast at the age of three, because his parents were also doing it. First, he was not a good player. So, he repeated practice very much. He could win games. When he got a silver medal in the Peking Olympics. He was very mortified, because he wanted to win the victory. He returned to Japan. Just then his mother said "Silver is better

*Photo courtesy of Rick McCharles on Flickr*

than gold." She sent a message for Kohei, because she wanted him to become fine again. He was encoured very much. He practiced hard again.

At first, he was not in a good condition in London. He fell from the iron bar. It is uncommon for him to fall, but he was supported by the teammate. So, they got some silver medals. However, it is not fun for Uchimura to lose to China. He tried to reduce mistakes, because he made some mistakes. Therfore, he could do the best performance. He got a gold medal in an event. I think that he made the utmost effort, since he won the victory in London Olympics.

First his tastes were intense to food. So he did not have some vegetables. When I heard it, I think that he is not a good player, because he ran away from his disliked things. But he did not give up. Yes, he is an ace, He tries to eat some vegetables, fish.... He became a strong body. I thought that it was OK

Uchimura said "I want to win a gold medal in my team. Probably, my thing is realizable.

I have been convinced, because, if they become No.1. they can prove that the Japan team is very strong. One more step, they could not become a champion, but, if there is no feeling of his the Japan team could not even get a medal.

I want them to win a gold medal in the next Rio Oliympic game:->!!! "Efforts are rewarded." He realized it by himself.

## Carp (baseball team)

This team is not rather popular in professional baseball teams, but, in Hiroshima, this team is loved by everybody.

This team uses many techniques. For example, this team often advances a runner on a bunt, executes a hit and run, and advance to third for a double steal. This team didn't get "A class" for a while. But this team might get "A class" this year! Why is this team strong this year? Because, this team should use many young men and they play an active part!

I think this team is a good team, but there is a bad thing about this team. This team is defeated successively and defeats successively. In short, this team is unstable.

This team is not popular in professional baseball team, but I cheer for this team.

# Books

# Hon

# 本

## Momotaro (NB. Peach Boy)

It's a tale of old Japan. The writer is unknown. It doesn't know when it was made.

Once upon a time, there was an old lady and an old man. He gathered fire wood. She did the washing in a river. She saw a huge peach rolling down the river. She took it out. Old lady and old man got to their house, and they would cut the peach. But, the peach burst open and there appeared the baby. They named him "Momotaro". He was very healthy. The more he ate, the bigger and stronger he became. At that time, demons attacked village. Momotaro decided to do something about the demons. He would go to demons' island and punish the demons. Old wife gave him kibi dumplings. On the way, he met a dog, a monkey and a pheasant. He gave them kibi dumplings. They accompanied him. They got to demons' island and fought the demons. They bite, scratched and pecked. The demons surrendered and gave them treasure. They returned safely and lived happily ever after.

It is most popular of the tales of old Japan. Japanese children hear this story in animation or picture-story show. Young and old people enjoy this tale. The story tells us that Justice always wins.

It is most popular and famous tale of old Japanese.

## Susanoo no Mikoto no Yamata no Orochi Taiji (NB. Susanoo no Mikato's Slaying of the Serpent)

This story is a Japanese myth. It is very popular. "*Susanoonomikoto*" is god like Hercules. "*Takamanohara*" is like Heaven. "*Yamatanooroch*" is a very strong dragon.

*Susanoonomikoto* is a very strong god, but he is hot-tempered. One day his sister, a godess, got angry with him, and he was exiled from *Takamanohara*. So he meets *Ashinazuchi* and *Tenazuchi*. They beg him to defend *Kushinadahime*, their daughter, from

*Yamatanoorochi*. After that he defends *Yamatanoorochi*, and he marries *Kushinadahime*.

This story is like Hercules of the Greek myths, by chance. Why it is the same? Everybody doesn't know. It is a mystery. This story is about rewarding good and punishing evil. We have a longing for a brave man.

## Sonezakisinzyu (NB. The Love Suicides at Sonezaki)

Sonezakisinzyu is popular in a Japanese puppet show and Kabuki. The story was written Chikamatsu Monzaemon in early Edo era. Lover's suicide booms in young people caused by Sonezakisinzyu. The government forbade it to commit a double suicide in a double suicide boom and took the measures that forbade the funeral of the people who committed suicide in 1723.   After that, revival of Sonezakisinzyu at Kabuki in1953, and a Japanese puppet show in 1955.

Soy sauce shop "Hiranoya" was served Tokube and a prostitute is Ohatu. They were loves of their lives. They were on the horns of a dilemma, love, justice, and money. They commit double suicide in Sonezaki Tenjin a wood.

Sonezakisinzyu is popular in Japanese literature.   The story has been printed in classic textbook. The story is express well life and mind of people in early Edo era.  Sonezakisinzyu is sad and painful love story, and an impressive story. I recommend Sonezakisinzyu in Japanese literature.

# Ryoma ga Yuku (Ryoma Goes His Way)
*Writer/Shiba Ryotaro*

Bakumatsu is the most important age for Japan. This novel is written about a man who played an active part in the Bakumatsu. This novel is popular because the novel was written about the age Japanese people have the most hopes.

This novel is a novel and a drama. This story is a fiction which was based on a historical fact. You can get on a bookstore. It is not so expensive.

We, Japanese are proud of our soul (we called it *Tamashi*) of "*Samurai*" or "*Bushi*" like chivalry. So I like this novel which makes me exciting. But it will be in the past only. This novel was written about Ryoma changed Japan. This person is popular with many Japanese.

For reading this book or watching this drama, you know important part of Japanese history. And this story is very exciting.

# Satan
*(2004), about 207 pages, Writer/Kotaro Isaka*

Kotaro Isaka is from Tohoku university, and he is a famous novelist in Japan. He wrote "A Coin-operated Locker of a Domestic Duck and a Wild Duck" and "Precision of the Got of Death". They are famous in Japan. He is a great novelist like Keigo Higashino.

Ando got an ability. It is the ability which makes a person say what he thinks. He thinks that Inukai, a politician, is a dangerous person. And he fights with different people to throw the politician with the power.

Because the story contains a lot of laughs, we can enjoy it. The story contains a sad scene, too. So we can feel sorrow. The story is variety. If you read the first part of this story, you will be fascinated by its interesting points. When you finish reading it, you will be satisfied with its interesting points.

It is difficult to read "Heat", the novel, which Soseki Natsume wrote. It contains a lot of difficult words. Though I have read it, I became tired when I had finished reading it. I think because he is an old novelist. However, "Satan" is easy to read. It doesn't contain any difficult words. When I had finished reading it, I didn't become tired. I think because he is a contemporary novelist.

A brave person fights with the politician in Japan.

## The Wind-up Bird Chronicle

*1997, Writer/Murakami Haruki*

This is a prize-winning novel, of the Yomiuri literature prize. This is a very interesting novel. The world is in 1984. A man named Okada met a lot of people. For example, sisters named

*Photo courtesy of Brew Books*

strange, a girl who doesn't go to school, a man who went to Nomonhan; there is a border town between Mongol and China, etc. Just then, he had a very large problem. He met a danger that he would get a divorce. Things around him changed one after another.

In 1984, Mr. Okada cooked spaghetti. Then, he was called a strange woman. Since then, he had gotten a lot of trouble. His wife, named Kumiko, left him one day. He met strange sisters named Maruta Kano and Kureta Kano. And Mr. Mamiya, who went to a war in Nomonhan. He got a blue bruise on his left cheek. This story is told very quickly. So it's difficult to explain, but this is a very interesting story.

This story has many characters. If you hear them all, you'll think "I can't remember!" But, all the characters' personalities are very strong. At first sight, I thought they have no relation, but there are a lot of relations at the final spurt. Then I was moved by the author's ability.

But this story is very long. So busy people, or a person who has no concentration, will not be able to read it. I want you to read it in a quiet room where there is no one. And this author said there are fit people and not fit people, for this book.

Murakami Haruki's story has a very unique world. So his story is loved all over the world.

← He is very happy.

# Fly, Dady, Fly
*2003, Writer/Kazuki Kaneshiro.*

Kaneshiro's other works are "revolution No.3", "SPEED" and "revolution No.0". The several male high school students links with these works. They are described as a supporting character not only a leading character. It is the rule of these.

The leading character's name is Hajime Suzuki. He has a daughter. A high school second-year student. The story begins on the day that she is taken to the hospital. Because a male student injured her. His name is Ishihara. She can't go away from fear. Suzuki decides that he fights with Ishihara for his daughter. But he is very weak to fight. So he asks to cooperate with the high school students, Minakata, Paku Sunshin, Yamashita, Itarashiki and Kanoya. Suzuki practices fighting with Suzuki for a month. When he can be ready to fight, the day come to do it with Ishihara. If you want to know this story's epilogue, I hope that you read this novel.

Mr.Kaneshiro has a good style. I am poor at reading a book. But his novel are easy to read and very interesting. Therefore it may be a boring book for adults. I think what a man is fighting student is a little strange. But this work is also the movie, so I want you to add it to your rental list.

This is a novel which you can feel the connection of family and friends.

# Knife of the Angel
*August 8, 2005, Writer/Yakumaru Gaku, Mystery novel*

This story won the Edogawa Ranpo prize. This story is said to have been outstanding in the selection society. *Knife of the Angel* is his debut nave

Hiyama Takashi is the protagonist. His wife was killed in front of her baby. But three of the criminals were boys, so that did not get punished. Four years later, out of the criminals was killed and Hiyama's innocence doubted. He looks for the truth.

This story gives doable hints which are to be developed later. Yakumaru Gaku makes use of a hint well and he never let us down. This book can be read at one go and we can return to reading it any number of times. The novel has two or three twists in the second half of the story. This novel is famous because it won a prize. His style drags us into his view of the world.

# Yamada Yusuke & Real Tag

He is writer. He was born in 1981. Many novels become the bestseller. He was born in 1981. He is from Tokyo. He graduated

from Yamato of Kanagawa City Minamirinkan Junior High School and Hiratsuka School Senior High School. From thought "to want to get work utilized the imagination in the future", he wrote a novel in parallel while living by a part-time job after graduation from High School. If anything, he seemed to dislike reading.

He makes my debut with a novel to describe a discriminatory theme including "the real tag" in 2001.The outline of this novel is the Christian era 3000 years. He heard announced the plan of "the real tag" that the king of a certain island caught national Sato Tsubasa (chief character) of the university student reading a newspaper and knew the news of the "the real tag". Can   Sato

Tsubasa resident in Yokohama and two people of younger sister, Sato Ai resident in Osaka survive? This novel is impressive till the last. Furthermore, I throb.

If I think, his novel's story is too much far apart from reality. However, therefore it is interesting. There are cruel scenes and the radical scene, but the scene of feeling for a friend and a family ties is included in that.

I like his novel. This is because it can feel a thrill very much. I intend to continue reading his novel from now on. In addition, I want everybody to read by all means. Surely it should be interesting.

## Juuni Kokki (NB. The Twelve Kingdoms)
*25th September, 1991, Writer/Huyumi Ono*

Juuni kokki is a fantasy novel. This novel is a masterpiece of huyumi ono. She is one of the most popular novelists. In japan. The turnover is over seven million and five hundred thousands copies. And this novel became TV animation. This novel is a serial story.

The main character is youko nakajima. She is an arerage high scgool student who is born and grows up in japan. Oneday The man wearing different clothes and calling himself "keiki" appears in front of her. Keiki calls yoko "king" and kneels to her. She is very surprised by unexpected occurrence. But suddenly the monster attack them. Narrowly Keiki put off assailing and keiki carries off youko to the another world. Tne plot is the first novels of serial story "shadow of moon, sea of shadow".

I think the good points of "juuni kokki" are two. First the heart felt description of character is very nice. This novel has a lot of characters. This novel draws the heart felt desscription of characters so fine. Second the novel a peculior world view. I think no one novel has a world view like

This novel is so interesting and stimulative. I think that everyone will enjoy this novel.

# The Man Sleeping Three Years

One day there is a man sleeping for three years. His mother takes care of him every day. But an inhabitant were always grumbing about the man and thinking they killed him. One day the town which the man sleeping was cave in. people lived in there were in trouble. Because grain of the fields will be dead. The then,

the man wake up. So he droped a storn from cliff to river. The storn damed up the river ,so the flow of water go to the fields of town. They were very happy and recognized him. Finally, he and the town helped each other.

I think that I like netarou{the man}. Because he helped the inhabitants. He gave trouble to them. For example, he was sleeping three years. He didn't worried. His mother support him. But, he helped with a crisis of the town. So," Everyone need in the world." "Never give up and belive in mine." It is very important. The story teach me them.

Netarou will helped people.

# Toaru Majutu no Index (NB. A Certain Magical Index)

"Toaru majutu no index" is popular with young people because this story is a school story and battle story.

This story world is super human ability solved for science. This hero is living the most advanced scientific city. The hero is a high school student. One day the hero meets hungry a Catholic nun. He help her and was heard about magic from her. He started his magic and science story.

This novel is congenial with me. I like science and magic. This novel mounts these topics. Science disagree with magic but this is the point of this novel. So this novel's hero is high school student. I like a school story. This novel's contents is very very very funny and give us deep impression. I can't explain this novel because it is very excellent.

Toaru majutu no index" is popular with young people because this story is a school story and battle story.

## Sword Art Online
*April 2009, Writer/Leki Kawehara*

Asuna, heroine from *Sword Art Online* shows her anime version figure, courtesy of Danny Choo

The novel started as an online novel in 2001, and had obtained high evaluation in 2004.And now, the number of exceeds 4,600,000. It is one of the novels representing Japan.

The story is an escape of impossibility and a game over means sure "death" until it clear ➙➙ With about 10,000 users who did not know the login "truth" of the next generation MMO of a mystery "Sword Art Online (SAO)". The severe death battle opened at the curtain. The hero is Kirito which is one person who participated in SAO and accepts the "truth" f the MMO promptly. And the cephalic angel was distinguished as a solo player which does not contract a party at the huge floating castle "Ainclad" used as stage of a game.

This "Sword Art Online" is the first novel I read. I think that this novel is the best things in several of these years. First, a hero is strong and smart. Probably, these are no such other novels like this with a strong hero. Second, I like the view of the world of the novel. Many boys have read this novel with pleasure.

This is very interesting and if it is read, it will be exiting. It is read by many people.

# Jigokudou Reikaitsuushin
*Writer/Kouduki Hinowa, Artist/Mimori*

It's Japanese monsters novel. All general people love this book. It's not popular. But,I don't know why. I think it is the most interesting in the would.

This book was written by Kouduki Honowa, and Mimori. Mimori is a cartoonist. So this novel became comics too. MIMORI can drew very beautiful picture. Probably comics are more popular than novels.

Only 8 novels are published and what is worse. Price is not good, a little bit expensive . Each one costs 1.000yen. Comics are the same. Each comics costs 6,00yen. Comics are about 5,00yen usually. So, I think these are expensive.

I love these books hero's.   Hero's are elementally school students.

Not only I am pretty, but also they are tender. Besides, There are very smart. However, they are ringleaders. Their name is the name called Tetsuhi, Shiina, Ryochinn.

I think this book should be more popular. I want people around the would to read books and see beautiful pictures .

# Dance with the Dragons
*Series, since 2003,Writer/Asai Labo.*

This is a realistic novel. The main characters aren't perfect heroes, they struggle against a lot of difficulties and reality.

There is a part that is a little cruel but we can get knouledge about science. There are two heros, Gayusu and Gigina. They are an bad teams but very strong when they fight together. One day,Gayusu and Gigina were involved in a big incident. After the case, They are dragged to many battles in succession. The enemies are dragons, monsters, giants and more. They are fighting against enemies to use "Jushiki"that manipulate all things in nature.

I think this novel is wonderful, because I like the chemistry assistance in this one. "Dances with the Dragons" said regular science. This massage is a little difficult, but this is one of it's charms.

In the second story, the main characters are ordinary people. They cann't become heroes but they are living. I think an ordinary people's story is rare. This story has a battle scene, too. A conbining battle and human drama are its interesting points.

It's a strange story. If you read this one,you will be captured.

## Weekly Boys Jump

*Made in Japan, Price: 240 yen/$3.20 USD / 2 GBP, A readership: A boy*

It is a very popular comic in Japan because it launches many funny comics title. For example, DRAGON BALL, NARUTO, BLERCH and so on. That title is living in our memories.

If you want to read it, you can go buy it every Monday. It is issued new number JUMP. Where can you buy it? We can buy any where!! A convenience store, A bookstore and A supermarket...because it is the most popular comic in Japan. There is not people who don't know it. Many people buy it Monday but you don't may fast go to buy. They want to read so shop keep many JUMP. But be careful! When we have holiday on Monday, it is issued on Saturday.

My family likes JUMP. I like also it so I buy it every week. My favorite comic title is "SKET DANCE". Its characters have humanity. They are high school students. So they laugh with their friends. Funny trouble and funny characters made us happy. But when they encounter many difficulties, they always put on a serious expression. We are electrified. But the main character got over his difficulties. They give us a courage!! There are many comics titles like SKET DANCE.

Its keywords are "A friend ship, A effort, A victory". If you read it, you can feel those and get inspiration.

## Dragonball

*(1984~1995), writer/Toriyama Akira.*

It is one of the most popular mangas in Japan, because the story is cool and charactors do hot battles. People involved; Son Goku, Kuririn, Son Gohan, Bejita,etc.

This story's hero is Son Goku. He is very strong and the peace of the earth is kept by him. This is a battle story and this story's hero is Son Goku. He kept the peace of the earth. He does hot battle with his rivals. This story carried from 1984 to 1995 and was released until vol.42. So to buy it is hard.

**(NB. Spoiler in the next paragraph!)**

This is a very exciting story. Especially, Cell's story is impressive. Son Goku is killed in this story. I worried. But his son, Son Gohan defeated Cell. This was a very hot battle.

The bad point of this story is that the drawing is old. I think these drawings should remake. But everyone should read it because the story is great. It is an exciting story. Everyone should watch this story

## Doraemon (1 of 2)

*Creator /Fujiko.F.Fujio, serialized since 1969.*

This work was made by Fujiko.F.Fujio. It is one of the juvenile comics representing Japan. The hero's name is Nobita. He can't do studying and sports. His model is the author (When he was young.) Doraemon is the cat robot which came from the 22$^{nd}$ century. Because he wants to help Nobita.

This work, which was extended, drew the everyday life of Nobita and Doraemon. Although the stage is the present age, it may go by time machine to the past or the future. Nobita's friends are Shizuka, Suneo, Takeshi. They also come as well. Takeshi's nickname is Jyaian. Doraemon takes out various secret tool.

I have known Doraemon since I was young. I liked it and watched it every week. The secret tool which comes out from Doraemon's pocket was really wonderful seeing the work is very interesting. This work delights adults and children. As a Japanese, I am proud of this work.

It is very populer in Japan. Doraemon is a famous comics. All Japanese know Doraemon.

# Doraemon (2 of 2)

Doraemon is popular because he is very exciting. His tools are very wonder and fun. He gives us

Not Doraemon

dream by the tools. Doraemon is a manga which is written by Fujiko.F.Fujio. Doraemon is a cat style robbot. But was bitten his ears by a rat, so he doesn't have ears. He is blue because he cried so much when he was bitten his ears.

He came to the present for the future to help Nobita. Nobita is a boy study and sports. He always bullied by Jaian. So Doraemon came to hear to help Nobita by using his tools. His tools are very wonder. For example, Dokodemoda ...the door which can go many places, Takekoputa ...it can fly in the sky etc. Nobita uses many tools when he has a hard time, and he become fine.

I think this story is very fun because Doraemon's tools make many people fine.

Naruto statue courtesy of aranmanoth on Flickr

# Naruto (1 of 2).
*Writer/Masashi Kishimoto.*

There are 62 books now. In the story, all characters are ninja. Ninja are people who work to make our countries good and safe. Naruto is populer because we japanese think ninja is cool.

The main character is Naruto. He is also a Ninja. This story is drawn around Naruto's growth through fighting and human relations. One day, his friend Sasuke suddenly went out of his country. Sasuke went to a bad person to be stronger. Naruto couldn't stop Sasuke. So Naruto tries to take Sasuke back now. This way Naruto not only works for his country but also tries to take his friend back.

I think this manga is a great story. If you read Naruto, you can be excited and learn friendship. I especially like the scene Naruto vs Sasuke. They were best friends, but they fought twice before now. Sasuke wants to kill his friend Naruto. Can Naruto help his crazy friend Sasuke ? I am excited.

Naruto is populer because it is an interesting story and we japanese think Ninja is cool.

## Naruto (2 of 2)

It is the story of "ninja" and the comic is a new style of ninja story. Naruto is a ninja school student. He is a troublemaker. So, he was not actually disliked by other student. No one cared that mach. He became famous as the worst student in the school. But he never gave up. Because of it, and he compete for rival, Sasuke, he grow up more and more as a ninja, as a human.

"NARUTO" is popular with teens. Because it can be read easily and the characters are almost the same age to us, school students. The scene of the fights makes us excited. I think there is the reason that it is popular.

The characters are different. My favorite character is Shikamaru. He is clever. He is shy, too. Because of his personality, he is believed by many ninja. It is the story of friendship of ninja.

## Shingeki no Kyozin (NB Giants Attack)
*Writer/ Isoyama Hazime.*

This manga's content original and interesting. One hundred years ago, suddenly giants appeared. Humans were attacked and were eaten, so humans built a very high wall which protected humans from giants.... But one hundred years later, The giant which is higher than the wall came and it broke wall, and giants ingressed on human's territory....

I think I never seen such a manga. The story is very serious and it has many mysteries. So I try to solve mysteries, and it is very interesting. The story has just started.

This manga is very interesting. So I want you to read this!

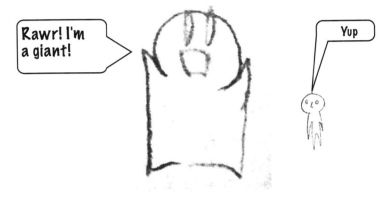

## Jojo's Bizarre Adventure

*Writer/Hirohiko Araki, Genre/Horror, Adventure, Released/August 10, 1987 (vol.1)*

The scene of the story is not only Japan but also UK, USA and Italy, and characters are foreign by nationality. This story has many characters who have a faith and are individual and cool and not seen elsewhere. And this story become the one and only in the world of its kind by combining them with individualistic picture.

JoJo is a battle manga that Banu Joestar battles against huge evil. Part1 "Phantom Blood" is Jonathan and Dio who is the vampire, part2 "Battle Tendency" is Joseph and Kars who is an Ultimate Thing, part3 "Stardust Crusaders" is Jotaro and DIO, part4 "Diamond is unbreakable" is Josuke and Kira who is a psycho killer, part5 "Golden wind" is Giorno and Diavolo who is a gang boss, part6 "Stone Ocean" is Jolyne and Pucci Fr., part7 "STEEL BALL RUN" is Johnny and Pres. Valentine, their battles are presented. Part8 "JoJolion" is serialized now.

At part1 and 2, the ability called "Hamon" appears, and at part3, the ability called "Stand". For example, ability which can close off (freeze) the time. These abilities are very individual.

I think that JoJo's charm is to enamor us to the characters. A lot of characters are presented and what life they have led in the story. They effect on their personality and belief. We feel that they live for real by knowing their life.

JoJo is the story of a long battle which crosses the generations. Heroes who defeat by brain and ability are very cool.

## JoJo's Bizzare Adventure Part IV
*Writer/Hirohiko Araki*

It's a Japanese comic. It's called "JoJo" by everyone. It has benn lasting now since 1987. The characters in this comic are very good. Also part IV has many characters everyone likes.

The story is developed in "Morioh twon". Higashigata Josuke, a popular name "JoJo", is the hero of the story. He spends strange days with his companions. They have strange ability—"stand". Stand has various kind. For example, repairing, putting everything into bomb and putting human into a book. They develop many battles with stand. At the last, Josuke fights to a killer, "Yoshikage Kira". It's very exciting.

My new friends.

JoJo's charm points are character and "stand". They makes us have fun, give strong impression, it's exciting, a joy. Especially, "stand" has merit nothing to others. The ability is very peculiar. It makes it better than other comics.

If you read this comic, you can get excited. And you will want to do "JoJo's standing".

## Atchikotchi (NB. Place to Place)
*(2006~), love comedy, Writer/Ishiki*

This comic has become popular recently becouse this was animeted. The heroine cannot be honest. Then hero is a blockhead. A reader will feel a frustrated sence of distance between he two. But it is the charm of this comic.

Certain stages of the story is at high school. The heroine's name is Tsumiki. She loves Io. Io is her classmate. He is at his own pace. He has to take care of her. But we don't know he loves her. Their friends Mayoi, Hime and Sakaki often enjoy to make fun of them. People around meddle in subtle sence of ditance of her two. We will want to watch two people get along with the characters surrounding.

I think it's a love-it-or-hate-it comic. I don't recommend to those who do not tolerate impatience. But I think it is the interesting work . I enjoy feeling impatient. I want you read once.

It is a popular romantic comedy comic which came out recently.

## Gingitsune (NB. Silver Fox)
*Released 18th September, 2009, Writer/Ochiai Sayori.*

I will have introduced Gingitsune . It is comics. It has popular because this story is good. This story is very tender. A lot of people said this story is interesting.

Main story is in temple. Makoto who is the only daughter at a temple, she lives in temple with her father and Gintaro (A messenger of God, he is fox). And Satoru. They are main characters. Other people can't see Gintaro. But Makoto and Satoru can see him.

I like this story. Because this story is very tender. I read it, and it makes me happy. Gingithune is said "good" by many people. I want to read this story.

Temples are very good! Let's read this! Gingitsune makes you very happy.

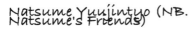

## Natsume Yuujintyo (NB. Natsume's Friends)

*Released 2003, Writer/Yuki Midorikawa*

Animation was carried out and it is already broadcast 5 seasons now. The comics are loved by many generations. The hero's name is Takashi Natsume. The story is a painful tale which begins with a hero looking at a supernatural creature. One day, a large supernatural creature's Madara(next Mr. Nyanko) are released. Natsume heard there is a "friend book" which is an article left by the departed Reiko. Natsume, a grandma. Natsume who understands Reiko's feeling returns the name to the supernatural creature, caught by the friend book. Natsume grows little in every day with Mr.Nyanko or other friends.

I think this is a very wonderful story. I have two reasons. First, here world which we can't experience usually is written. Although, the supernatural creature may exist, we can't understand it. It's a tale in which we can feel the wonder and fearfulness. Second, the change of mental state of Natsume and other is drawn very delicately.

When Natsume, the hero, was young, he was bulled by his friend, and the supernatural creature was also disagreeable, but he becomes a high school student, he meets a kind person and Natsume himself becomes gentle. I love this story so much.

This tale is a heart-warming thing, truly. Natsume's tenderness called people's sympathy.

# Lupin III

This work has made a new story every year since 1967, but it's not felt old. Then it is an easy to understand a story and its characters are very attractive.

Lupin the third, Arsene Lupin's grandchild, is very active as a thief with Daisuke Jigen, a quick shooter and the others running away from Zenigata, ICPO's police officer.

*Lupin III figure courtesy of Fernando Marcelino on Flickr*

This work was released in comic books and DVDs. This work is intended for adult and it's impossible to divide gentle because it contains action, comedy, hard-boiled detective, nonsense, and erotic thomes. So it should not be seen by children.

# Crayon Shinchan

*Released 1990~2010, Writer/Yoshito Usui, 50 volumes, Gag.*

"Shinnosuke" and other people make us laugh and impress them. The comic is popular with a child and an adult because characters are individual.

These comics are that getting into mischief impudent 5 years old child is hero. His name is "Shinnosuke Nohara". This is that they are comics of gags to which his parents and other people are perplexed in the disturbance which he causes.

These comics give us laughter and impression. His mischief makes us laugh and he is going to help his family and his friend impresses us. I think that I'm helpful in order that these comics may know the importance of bonds.

If these comics are read, laughter and impression can be got and the importance of bonds can be known.

## Miracle Ball

*Writer/Nagatoshi Yasunori, Baseball comedy*

It is very popular manga because it made a deep impression on us. Children become adults until they think about baseball and effort.

It is a story I am able to laugh at, and to be able to sometimes cry. The story that the Musashimaru second junior high school which is baseball club of the weakest type challenges the strongest Musashimal first junior high school to a game. The baseball club must be dissolved if they lose a game. The team which was unskillful becomes gradually good. I think Miyamoto Fumetu and Sasaki Kyuziro are the best pitcher and catcher.

I learned the importance of making on effort through these comics. I want to always have a feeling to give up on nothing.

Why don`t you cause a miracle!!!!!!

## Bokurano (NB. Ours)

*Writer/Kito Mohiro*

This comic appeared as a series that was run in a monthly magazine IKKI. The anime was broadcast in April 2007 by GONZO animation film production company.

Fifteen boy and girl of junior high school took a trip to an island as learning through practical experience. There, they met a mystery man in a cave. He suggested a "game". Details of the "game" is too simple. It is a fight , robot to robot ,to defend the earth. The pilot is them. But the robot of energy is their life! They must choose either two selection.   "Defending for the earth, you die." Or "Not defending for the earth, you die." A fifteen boy and girl considers this problem.

When I read this comic at the first time, I was shocked. If I am in the situation. What would I do? I will probably not do anything and die. But thirteen years old children younger than me do anything for action. One person is at a loss not to accept. Another person fights to protect his family. The change of mind in the story is the charm.

I think this story is gloomy. So if you read it, you should be careful. But it is very interesting.

**Wrong robot**

## WORKING!!

*Writer/Takatsu Karino, Released 2005, comedy*

The title of the manga is WORKING, but the character is not working very hard. Cartoon characters work at a restaurant. This story is set in Hokkaido. The characters have a strong personality. Main characters are like girls of twelve and under. There are only twelve people and over around the characters.

It goes without saying that this manga is interesting. You cannot help laughing if you read it. I think WORKING!! is worth buying. My favorite character is Inami Mahiru. She is weak in man and hit man in spite of herself. She tries to overcome it. I think she is pleasant her attitude to it.

This manga is to be continued. I look forward to continuance.

Cosplay Rurouni Kenshin courtesy of Regis Andrade on Flickr

## Rurouni Kenshin (NB. Wandering Sword)

*Released 1994, Writer/Nobuhiro Wathuki*

It is comics which has a story of Japanese Samurai. In this comic, characters are cool and also their feats are exciting and cool. But this story is not only exciting and cool, but also impressive.

Many persons of the Edo era and Meiji era enter these comic. The stage of this story is from Bakumathu to Meiji Ishin. A hero of this story is Kenshin Himura. He is a samurai who has a great technique. He has been called Hitokiri Battosai. He killed many people till the new age. When met the new age, he had stopped killing people. He decided to defend people without killing. People who hate him will kill him and his friends. So he must defend them.

The story of other main characters is depicted as an important part. Their lifestyle, belief and the past are drown. So reader can penetrate this comic deeply. They must fight against many strong persons. Every it, they deepen bands. Reading this comic, we ought to feel various things. This comic is not only interesting.

It is a great comic which is also exciting and dramatic. Both drawing and the story are great.

## ☆Kimi to Boku☆ (NB. You and Me)

*Released 2003, Writer/Kichi Hotta*

Kimi to Boku began with a four-frame comic strip. It became its own comic later and became the animated cartoon. The main characters are two people, Akira and Koich. They have known each other since we were small children. Koich became the teacher of the high school. Then, his student a group of four becomes a main character. The comic draws ordinary high school life of them.

When Akira and Koich became high school students, they went to the kindergarten in workplace experience. At that time, a group of four whom they met was Yuta, Yuki Kaname and Shun. And these four people become high school students. Furthermore, two new friends join these four people. The high school life that is their youth is in this story. The comic is released in 11 volumes, (One costs ￥419/$5 USD/3 GBP). The animated cartoon is 26 episodes.

This comic is very fun. I think it makes everyone interested. Particularly, I will collect the comics fun. My favorite scene is the conversation with Yuki, Chizuru and Kaname. Many jokes and laughter does not stop. However, I may feel the bond of the friends. Kimi to boku is my favorite comic. Interesting high school life is described in this comic. It is a Youth gag comics.

## Kids on the Slope
*Released 2007*

It was published serially from 2007 through 2012. It was broadcasted as an animated cartoon in 2012. It is drawn about jazz and love. Particularly,the scene to play music is splendid. Beautiful music and energetic pictures us.

Kaoru Nishimi is a high school boy. He changes school to the high school in Nagasaki. He was not used to the dialect and a classmate. He met Kawabuchi Sentaro. Sentaro is quarrelsome and is tyrannical. Kaoru was not used to him. One day, Kaoru found that Sentaro likes jazz and plays the drums. Kaoru often played classical music on the piano. But Kaoru found the charm of the jazz steadily and plays it with Sentaro.

I like the scene to play jazz. Particularly. I want to push forward to the scene of the school festival. It is the scene that Kaoru is reconciled with Sentaro. But they don't talk. They exchange feelings by using the music as words. Beautiful melody of piano, energetic rhythm of drum, hlarmonious performance, they are splendid. However, not only the performance but also the picture is excellent. Their figure to play the jazz impresses me. It is like summer and a lemon and the sea.

It is the story that two boys are playing jazz.

The ground is not level

### Hana Yoridango (NB. Riceballs over Flowers)

*Released 1992 – 2004, Girl`s comic, vol. 1-37*

A heroine: Tukushi, A hero: Domyoji. Hana yoridango was made into a drama and a movie when I was a child. The theme song of a drama and a movie had been popular in Japan.

Tukushi entered the Eitoku gakuen high school. This school is richer than other school. But she was born poor. One day, she met a good-looking guy, who belonged to a group. This group is called "F4". Domyoji is F4`s leader. He fell in love with Tukushi. So Tukushi`s school life was changed...!

Tukushi has a strong heart because she walks her way with Domyoji and her friends. I like the last scene. Tukushi looking back upon a memory. She is dancing with her friends. I want to read the sequel to a comic. I like Tukushi and Domyoji.

Love is the most important thing around the world! Not money!

### Pokémon Adventure

*Writers/Hidenori Kusaka,* Satoshi Yamamoto, Mato

Because this comic is Pokemon story. Pokemon is one of the famous games in the world.

This comic has been released to the 41. There are a total of 9 chapters, followed by a new chapter today. Each has attractive heroes. Also Pokémon's are sometimes cool and cute. The story is exciting and impressive. Each story is interesting for people who like Pokémon.

First, I think that this comic is the best comic about Pokémon. Pokémon adventure has been serialized since 15 years ago. It is amazing! Second I like Pokémon, I've been playing the game so I'm interested in the comic. This comic help me to play the game for knowing about Pokemon's real story and enjoying the game.

Cartoon was a good representation of the world of Pokémon.

## Eria no Kishi ( NB. The Knight in the Area)

Writer/*Igano Hiroaki, Tukiyama Kaya*

I am excited for it to be realistic deployment. It feels a familiar love story is also not just about soccer. It is also professional soccer player acclaim.

The hero is Kakeru. He had been yearning to his brother Suguru. They were involved in an accident. Suguru is dead, Kakeru was seriously injured. Kakeru survived by Suguru's heart transplant. Kakeru decided to continue to play soccer for the dream that did not true for Suguru.

I think it will be fun to read this more in soccer stories. There is a sense of reality, such as if you are playing with me in the book too. The art is very cool. It show many soccer games. I really enjoy the hero or what kind of growth he has.

I think it is a popular reason that we can enjoy soccer by reading it.

## Hajime No Ippo (NB. Fighting Spirit)

*Released 1990, made by Morikawa George.*

Hajimeno No Ippo is a comic which has been serialized since 1990. It has been published until 100 volumes. It felt presence and force of boxing.

Makunouti Ippo was bullied by bad students. Takamura Mamoru, who is a boxer helped him then. He wanted to change, so he began boxing. He always searches to "what is strong?" So he fights very strong boxers.

It is very interesting, exciting and invigorating. Because his game is very cool, exciting and powerful. I was impressed by his efforts and his figure which is not giving up. It teaches important of friendship and efforts. I think it is a popular reason that we can enjoy boxing by reading it.

## Death Note

Death Note is important in Japan because it became movie. This movie was released also overseas. However , the comics are not famous.

Photo courtesy of Mr. Cacahuate on Flickr

"The person is die who was wrote this note." (NB The person whose name is written in the notebook will die) is the biggest rule. Raito Yagami is one of the people to get the note. He thinks the person who committed a big crime should be dead. Later he was called "Kila" by anther people.

There is who was called him "L". He want to catch "Kila". So starting the two men`s war.

When I read Death Note, I made to think by this work. It`s the person who committed heavy crime. Beginning I considered it him the same think. If you read this work, you cannot but consider this story.

I want more many people to read this work.

## Crows

*Writer/ Hirosi Takahasi.*

This is a manga drawn about the bad boys. Many people long for this cartoon character. Adults read this cartoon, there may be remembered that be young.

Harumiti Boya is hero who trans ferred in Suzuran boys high school. Then he stacked the fight with various odds and foster friendship.

I was reading this, I knew the importance of friends and was struck by the friendship doesn't think bark risk. If you read this you will know ture friendship

# Slam Dunk

*(1990 - 96), Writer/Takehiko Inoue*

Slam Dunk is a very popular comic because basketball comics were rare then, it was fresh. All of the people longed to ve a basketball player and the characters of the comics make wise remarks. The words have become famous.

Sakuragi Hanamichi is a protagonist, he is a first year high school student. He starts the basketball club from high school. He plays frantically the first time. But he gives full play to his talent little by little. His high school plays the game with all sorts of other high schools. And they have an eye on domination of Japan.

I read the comic books and watched the animation. I thought that youth is very wonderful. I like the characters, because they have passionate devotion to play basketball. I learned thoughtfulness and enthusiasm from the comics. There are plenty of a basketball comics now, but I think that Slam Dunk is the best.

The comic makes a really deep impression. You should read the comics at any cost.

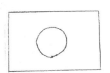

Animation

Anime

アニメ

# The Anpanman (1 of 2)

*Writer/Takashi Yanase*

Anpanman is a very popular anime in Japan. Because a lot of very cute characters are popular with children.

*A regular, non-magical anpan courtesy of My Blue Van on Flickr*

Anpanman is anime. It is very interesting and a very cute anime. The main characters are Anpanman, Shokupanman and Currypanman. Anpanman and Baikinman fought for the peace. If Anpanman lost, Jamojisan bakes bread. Jamojisan makes the Anpanman's face. Then Anpanman makes a recovery then!

I thought, Anpanman should spread all over the world. Because Anpanman is a great anime. Almost all Japanese children watch it.

Anpanman is very popular anime in Japan. Because many people watched it when they were children. I like it. I want to go to Anpanman museum in Sendai.

# Soreike! Anpanman (2 of 2)

This anime is known to have a lot of characters are attractive. It is registered with Guinness.

Anpanman is a symbol of justure (NB. Justice). Other people are attracted by his flying.  This anime was born in 1969. But, it improved. So, "Soreike! Anpanman" was completed in the present in 1975.

This anime's hero is "Anpanman" his face to the children who are crying because they are hungry. So, he is kind enough to sacrifice his face. While, the main villain is "Baikinman" against "Anpanman" of justice hero. He always gets into misthief. Many children cried to be builled when the sweet was thieved. "Anpanman" helps them to defeat "Baikinman"----------This story is always constituded.

My opinion is that "Anpanman" defeat "Baikinman". "Anpanman" wins by how he fights with the punch or kick and quickly. This ways is wrong because young children are educated to be bad them. Certainly. "Baikinman" bullys a lot of people. This is never allowed to be. But, "Anpanman" should talk out the problem. He always breaks "Baikin UFO". "Baikinman" flies for away. At this time, "Baikinman" is strong, he never dies. A normal person dies. Maybe he is done just because he is strong? But, no. "Anpanman" should

solve problems without "Baikiman" damaged.

I morn over the loss each time and do not stop. "Mr.Ynase", Thank you for enjoying me. I have watched "Soreike! Anpanman" every

week until now.

## Digimon (1 of 2)
*Released in 1999.*

It is easy for us to be familiar with it because the characters are cute and cool. And the scale in this animation's, comic's, games are very grand. So, we love "Digimon."

One day the children will enter a computer's program. There it is called "Digital world." Many creatures are living there. The creatures called "Digimon.' They have feelings and act alone. The children will meet them and adventure together.

"Butter-fly" is the first animation's opening song. This song is very tender and powerful. So, this song is so match with the animation.

I think this animation is wonderful because we can feel their bonds through their adventure. I want to follow their movement. So, I think this animation is wonderful. By the way, I also like "Pokemon" but they can't talk. And they can evolve but they can't degenerate. But "Digimon" can talk and degenerate. So, I like it better than "Pokemon." My particularly favorite character is "Agumonn." It is "Digimon" looks like a dinosaur. Agumonn's ultimate form is very cool and strong. So, I like "Agumonn." I want you to like "DIGIMONN."

Children will enter a place called "Digital world." Then, they will adventure over there by meeting the creatures called "Digimon."

## Digimon Adventure (2 of 2)

This is an anime. The last is very impressive. Digimon Adventure is loved by a lot of people for a long time.

Suddenly, seven children (Taichi, Yamato, Sora, Koshiro, Jo, Mimi and Takkeru )go to File Island in 1999 August first. They have a partner Digimon. When the children are in danger, Digimon can evolution. Digimon become stronger and defeat many enemy. When last enemy defeat, they go real world.

This anime is so good. I have watched since I was a kindergarten child. This anime show us bonds with friends and life importance. Opening song is "Butter-Fly" This song is sung by Wada Koji. Butter-Fly is also loved by many Digimon fan. Ending songs are "I Wish" and "Keep On" They are sung by Maeda Ai. These songs are nice.

Digimon Adventure is very good anime. Opening song and Ending songs are very nice. Digimon is better than pokemon.

## K-ON! (1 of 2)

The model for K-ON! is high school life, so it is popular with young people. K-ON!'s characters are very cute. There are many fans of them.

*K-ON figures in a photo courtesy of Danny Choo*

This anime's theme is high school life. There are five girls in it. The names of them are Yui, Ritsu, Mio, Mugi, Azusa. They belong to the band club. They always practice different songs. The songs are very nice. My favorite song is "Don't say lazy".

This anime's original version is manga. This manga was sold to young people. In Japan, This anime's DVD is sold in the DVD shop. We can borrow them at a low price.

This anime is very nice. I am not interested in anime but I like it. Other animes don't make me feel interested. This anime is special. I don't get tired when I am watching this anime. You should watch this anime once.

My favorite character is "Ritsu". She is very positive so I'm fine when I saw her. But Ritsu is not popular. It's very sad. Mio and Azusa are very popular.

I bought DVDs of this anime but I don't have manga of it. I don't like to read books. My friends say "This anime's manga is very interesting". So I want to read this anime's manga. Please read Japanese manga once.

It's popular with young people. We can feel interesting and I think you can be interested in this anime.

## K-ON! (2 of 2)

This animation is popular with young people because the original songs is popular with young people. This animation is about five girls who are belong to the band club. This story is of their daily activities. Yui, Ritu, Mio, and Mugi are 12th grades. Azusa is an 11th grader. They are members of "Houkago Tea Time". Their main activities are practicing music.

I am fond of this story. Their school life is so interesting. Though the story is only real , it makes me cheerful. Yui is slight fool. Ritu is captain of the band club. Mio is cool. Mugi is my pase (NB. she's very easygoing but a bit ditzy). Azusa is called Azunyan. They enjoy their own life.

My favorite original song is "Huwa Huwa Time". I often listen to the music with my music player. The song makes me happy. I think it's a very exciting animation.

## Sazaesan

*Writer / Hasegawa Mathiko*

Sazaesan started 1946. Most Japanese know it. People say this anime is very interesting.

Sazaesan is a house wife. Her family is big. There are seven people in her family. Her family

The cast of Sazaesan represented in snow at the Sapporo Snow Festival, Hokkaido, Japan.

has many troubles. For example, her brother doesn't study. They father is very angry, but they find a solution to it every time. The characters are very warm and interesting.

This animation is very interesting. I was very warm when I saw it. This animation is very kind. So this makes many people happy. On Sunday many Japanese see it. Many people look for it.

It is very warm. This doesn't make us sad. This animation goes perfectly with a Sunday.

## Tensai Bakabon (NB. Genius Bakabon)

*Published in 1967, writer / Akatuka Fujio.*

It is funny tale. It has many interesting characters. Main chracters are Bakabon and Bakabon's father. Bakabon's father was a genius. But some accidents made him foolish. His character is not only interesting, but also inoccent. Other characters are Hajime, Bkabon's mother,and Rererenoojisann etc.

They bring about a lot of things make us funny. I saw it for the first time when I was ten. I thought "It is funny". Akatuka Fujio is very talented. It is one of the best cartoons. So it never fails to make us laugh.

# "C" - The Money Of Soul And Possibility Control

Possibly, this is not popular. But I think "C" is the most exciting anime in recently times.

In 20xx, Japan. The Japanese economy slowly restore. But, stranger troubles and suicide has happened one after another. The people cannot get the favor. Kimimaro Yoga is an economic univercity student. He is a working student. One day, [We will furnish you with fands. But your future make this collateral] a strange man said to Kimimaro. This is the start of "C". Please enjoy yourself with this animation's DVD!

This animation's best charm point is "Battle and Charactor". A technical term of financial circles appears in the work. as a charactor`s skill. It is so cool. And the official site. explained it. This works director is absorbed in the back grounds design. Opening and Ending music and movie make me excited. And more, tempo of work is good too. But I regreted that `C` is too short astory. On the contrary, you can enjoy in short time.

This story has a lot of charming point. Fantasy, battle, reality, boy meets girl, conflict ....

Please watch.

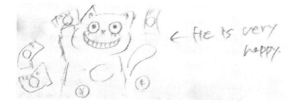
← He is very happy.

## Mobile Suit Gundam

All robot anime so for has been about the growth of the mind of the protagonist, drawing the difference, war and since it is realistic, this anime was popular with adults more than children. In this story there is the concept of a "New Type". It is a revolutionary, who was born in the future of mankind.

It said that too many people who have immigrated to the human race in the universe, so on earth there are those who were born there but are not earthlings. Revolutionary war happened for the earth. This is where this story takes place. The side of the earth, where there are military heroes, the earth side will win in the end though.

Mobile Suit Gundam has become a lot of series. It is the same story with any war that is taking place now. I hope I should have thought about the war.

## Hello Kitty

Hello Kitty is very popular with Japanese people, because Kitty is cute. Kitty is loved by adults, not only children.

Hello Kitty is a Sanrio character. Kitty's real name is Kitty White. Kitty is cat that was born in London. Kitty like apple pie made by her mother . And, goods made by Hello Kitty, for example stationery, clothes, confectionery. I like those very much.

When I was a little, I saw a Hello Kitty for the first time. I have been loved Hello Kitty since then. Kitty is the most popular Sanrio character. Because Kitty is very cute . I want to know about Hello Kitty in the world. I think Kitty will always be popular.

Kitty is a Sanrio character. It is very cute and popular with Japanese people. I want to know about Hello Kitty in the world.

*Hello Kitty nail art courtesy of pumpkincat210 on Flickr*

# Dear Daniel

*(1999), Sanrio company, Director / Yuko Yamaguchi*

"Dear Daniel" was made by Yuko Yamaguchi who Sanrio's artist. She also made "Hello Kitty". "Dear Daniel" was born in 1999 as Kitty's boyfriend. He has been loveing all over japan with "Hello Kitty" for long time.

"Dear Daniel" — his real name is "Daniel Ster". a Sanrio's character

of a white cat boy. Sanrio have a charactor who the most popular in Japan, we call har "Hello Kitty". She is a white cat girl. Daniel is her boyfriend. He is a sentimental and naïve boy. Daniel was on good terms with Kitty, but when he was little boy, he moved to Africa with his family for his father's work. They couldn't meet for a long time. But before long he came back to London for Kitty. His hobbies are dancing, playing the piano and taking pictures. He wants to become an entertainer or a photographer.

I think "Dear Daniel" is should be loved all around the world. Because he is very charming boy. When I saw him at the first time, I feel he look kind and smart. In Sanrio Puroland, a theme park produced by Sanrio studio, he is playing an important part in a musical, show and attraction. I believed that he will give us happiness and a good impression. "Dear Daniel" is very charming boy.

TV

Terebi

テレビ

# Taiga Drama
*NHK*

A Taiga Drama is a Japanese historical drama. It is broadcast at 20:00 every Sunday. All generations of people watch our history.

Taiga Drama is a personal drama. This drama's story is the life of a person who did great works many years ago. And this story is broadcast during a year. In other words, the story is changed every year. This year's drama is "Tairano Kiyomori." It is a person's name. He did a lot of great works in Japan's history. We can learn traditional Japanese culture very much by watching it.

I like this drama very much! My favorite drama is "Ryomaden." It's Japanese revolutionary, Ryoma Sakamoto's story. Watching it not only makes me excited but also gives me knowledge. I learned many parts of Japanese history. In the past, there were a lot of dramas about Japanese princess, Samurai and so on. Now, I watch it every Sunday and learn a new part of Japanese history.

It is a long drama about a person who did great works. And we can learn Japanese history and traditional culture by watching it.

# MASKED RIDER OOO
*September 5th 2012- August 28th 2011, TV Asahi, 30 minutes long. Director:/Ryuta Tasaki, Writer/Yasuko Kobayashi, Stars/Shu Watanabe, Ryosuke Miura, Riho Takada etc.*

MASKED RIDER OOO is one of the MASKED RIDER Series. And the twelfth Heisei MASKED RIDER Series. OOO's toy "DX OOO Driver" recorded the best sales then of all MASKED RIDER's toys.

The fall of 2010 monsters called "Greed" was awakened from the sleep of 800 years. But there was a man who does not even notice such things. His name is Eiji Hino. He is a young man of unselfish wandering the world. One day, Ankh appeared before the eyes of

Eiji. He was one of the Greed, was the right arm. "Yummy" Greed has created monster suddenly there has been attacked. Eiji confronted in order to protect people. Ankh saw it and passed on to the belt and medals Eiji. Eiji transformed into himself "MASKED RIDER OOO" and defeated Yummy. Eiji determined to fight this way as OOO. Meet allot of fellows, he got "infinite bond" time. However, since all cracked his medals, Ankh has disappeared. But, in the last moment, while immersed in the "highest satisfaction", he said to thank to Eiji. After the battle, Eiji has traveled to the world again. With cracked Ankh's medal.

SFX was used in many scenes. Especially battle image was very cool. Also, every episode was interesting. My best episode is the final episode. It was very impressive. But one episode was decreased in time because of the disaster of March 11th, 2011. It was regrettable thing. I think many foreigners can enjoy watching MASKED RIDER OOO.

Eiji fights to stop Greed's ambition. Ankh fights with Eiji to get his medals and to regenerate perfectly. Their purposes were different, but they were bound strong confidence. Finally they got things that they had wanted each other.

## SPEC (1 of 2).

*Director/Tsutsumi Yukihiko, the others. Writer/Nishiogi Yumie, Stars/Toda Erika, Kase Ryo*

SPEC is a drama serial (2010), SPEC SYO is a one night drama(2012), SPEC TEN is a movie screened(2012), SPEC KETSU will may be screened someday.

SPEC is a special ability, for example, to stop time, movie so fast, possess humans, erase memories, heal symptom, and so on. A little human who have SPEC struggle in japan. The detectives fight against these humans. And solve these unknown affair. Finally, they fight a boy who can stop time!

Exceeding humans ability limits is exciting. A clever detective who can fight against SPEC is also exciting for me.

SPEC is a TV drama and a movie. I'd like you to watch both of them. It will surely excite and impress you.

# SPEC (2 of 2)

This story includes a lot of humor. For example, there are other TV program's parodies in it. The character is crazy. But SPEC isn't only humor. There are serious scenes too. The battle scene is very powerful. The character's life is complicated. These differences made SPEC popular.

It is said that the human's brain doesn't use itself perfect. It's only used 10%. But there are special humans that can use it. They are called "SPEC HOLDER". For example, they can use Time stop, Psychomety, etc. But some of them use it for bad things. The police officer, Toma and Sebumi are against them. They are a bad pair, but sometimes, they look the best pair. Presently, two persons know a big crisis which will control world destiny. They battle the SPEC HOLDERs organization.

What will two persons do on meeting? Peace? Are there a lot of battles? ――――World end?

This story spreads out of the TV program. It is made into a movie, a comic, a novel, and a mobile phone's game. And there is the American version SPEC's plan. It spread to the world.

I think this story is very typical, because sometimes, the humor isn't simple. The story is complicated. It may separate people's likes and dislikes. It suddenly changes to serious scenes and comedy scenes. So, some people may be not adapting to it. But I like the character is tics and differences. I got used to it there, and I think it's funny. If you feel "I can't endure it.", please watch this story a little more. You must know the interest soon.

An unforeseen story gives us excitement and a laugh. You should see this story!

## Dear Water Boys.

Water Boys is popular with the young generation. The reason is that this story make us happy. Water Boys is a movie and a diorama. This story has three series.

This story's leading role is high school boys who are members of a swim team. But they couldn't swim fast. So they gave up swimming. In the next series, they started a synchronized swimming loam of man. Then they made an effort to succeed at the school festival.

I like the Water Boys series. Especially, I like Water Boys two, too. I feel that the story has youth and love. So I think that the acting of the story is very hard. I was impressed by it, too. I want everyone to watch Water Boys.

# Movies

# Eiga

# 映画

# Hayao Miyazaki

Born in 1941.In Tokyo His occupation is animation author comic artist. His picture and construction are very good and interesting. His work's name is "Ghibli" movie is famous in the world. His representative movies are "Totoro", "Mononoke" and others. He has many works and there are all good as movies. His comic is "Nausica". His novel is a "Laputa". He has many awards for these works. They are the most of worldwide reputation awards.

*Photo courtesy of Loren Javier on Flickr*

I think he has splendid talents. So, I like the best movies of the author is Hayao Miyazaki. His movies are all interesting for me and I like them. I think, he wants to tell us to hide in his movie. He tells us through somebody about his movie. So, I will be a fan and have great expectations of his work.

# Laputa: Castle in the Sky (1 of 2)

*Released on 2 August 1986 (Japan), 124 minutes, animation, adventure. Director/Hayao Miyazaki, Studio Ghibli*

This animation is the first one for studio Gibli. I think the reason this is a popular animation is that we are so excited by the adventures of the heroes.

One night, the girl came down slowly from the sky with light. Pazu, working in the mines, hid at home to help her, Seeta. "Laputa: Castle in the Sky" was seen by Pazu's deceased father. They decided to go to Laputa because of Sheeta is a descendant of the people of Laputa and her pendant is from Laputa. Helped with the robbers of the sky, Dola family, they arrived at castle in the sky. And they try to stop Muska who would abuse power of Laputa.

This animation is still loved by people 26 years after release. The reason for this is that we want to watch it again and again. I think so. This work is a work that we can watch many times and it lefts me taste the same excitement and inspiration from when we saw it for the first time. Castle in the sky is mysterious and you are excited by what you see. The presence of this castle is a different with the other adventures.

It is an adventure story in which a boy and a girl go to a "Castle in the sky."

## Laputa:Castle in the Sky (2 of 2)

*Laputa statue photo courtesy of Spinster Cardigan of Flickr*

The first animated cartoon original which means there is not a previous work becoming the original movie. 1 item of the production of the Studio Ghibli. A character is individual and interesting. Musuka is the most popular in this movie. I like him.

The main character are Pazu, Sita, Dora, and Musuka. Pazu who is a chief character. One day Sita fell from the sky to Pazu. Musuka colonel who is an enemy, aimes at her because she has a flight stone. It is the thing which moved Laputa. Using it, Musuka plots would conguest. Pazu, Sita, and Dora confront it in order to stop it.

I like this movie. No, I love the movie! This movie is interesting and impressed me. And he characters do it lively. A Ghibli movie has a purpose. I think this movie shows the case for the environmental problem and concern for the nuclear weapon. In such a meaning, I think that the movie which is an important thing is in order for admiration. So I continue supporting it from now on.

## Tonari no Totoro (My Neighbour Totoro)

*88 minutes long, animation, fantasy. It was released on 16th April 1988 (Japan) Director/Hayao Miyazaki*

"Tonari no Totoro" is created in a beautiful countryside. This film is made by STUDIO GHIBLI. It is the same team that created "Kaze no Tani no Nausika" (Nausica of the Valley of the Wind).

The Totoro statue at Ghibli museum courtesy of Koroshiya on Flickr

Many lives are living in the countryside. But there are living things that you have never seen in this movie. It is time for Kusakabe's family to move to Tokorozawa. Their house was old, and there was a very big tree near the house. Mei of four and Satuki of twelve are sisters. They met "Totoro", a very big and pretty monster there. Totoro had a strange ability. Mei and Satuki experienced many interesting with Totoro. Except for Totoro, there are many living things. For example,"Nekobasu"(cat bus) shaped like a cat and bigger than Totoro. Nekobasu transports Totoro to the other pleces. But who can see them ? Only children.

This movie tells us Japanese beautiful nature and the bond of family. Their characters ,who appear in this movie, was considering their family all through the movie. It is good movie for children.

My favorite part is the scene that Mei was lost her way and Satuki was looking for she. Please you watch this movie with your family.

This movie is a fantasy that is written about two small girls who met the big monster.

## Tonari no Totoro (2 of 2)

To tell the truth when "Tonari no Totoro" was shown for the first time, it wasn't very popular, but after that this movie was broadcast many time because "Totoro" become a symbol of "Studio Ghibli". By the way, a film director, who directed "Toy Story", John Lasseter says "This movie is the most favorite movie in my life!"

This story is set in Japan in the age without TV (probably about 1950s.) The sisters, Satsuki and Mei have moved to a rural town from a city with their father. Their mother is sick so she is in a hospital. Satsuki and Mei enjoy living there! They meet strange creatures. Such as a ghost of soot "makkuro urosuke", a very big and cute monster "Totoro" and so on. One day they hear good news! Their mother will come back home but this good news changes bad news. She gets out of condition and can't return home. Satsuki runs to call to hospital. Then Mei follow her and lost her way.....

I think this movie is loved by many people (children, adults, old people and everyone!) There are two reasons. First, we can see many views of the countryside. So most adults will feel nostalgic and remember their home town. When I saw this movie for the first time, I was a young child but I longed for rural life. Second, the characters are very popular and cute. Especially "Totoro" is the most popular of all characters. In fact, about 30years have passed since this movie was shown but it's character's goods are still popular with many people.

This is a heart-warming and a little wonderful story about a meeting of two sisters and "Totoro". The catch phrase is "This strange creature is still in Japan. Probably." I think so too.

## Kiki's Delivery Service
*Released 1989, Director/Hayao Miyazaki*

Kiki's Delivery Service was made by Studio Ghibli. Studio Ghibli made a lot of animation movie. For example, My Neighbor Totoro. Hayao Miyazaki is a very famous director and illustrator around the world.

Kiki is a young witch. When she was thirteen, she went on a trip to "Koriko" to be a good witch. She met "Osono" who is a baker in there. She helped the bakery and started a delivery service. She flew by broom to deliver the package. By the way, Kiki has a boy friend.

His name is Tonnbo. He is interested in airplanes. One day, Tonnbo was put in danger by a strong wind. Kiki went there to help Tonnbo.

The movie's story is very interesting but background music is one of the most famous in Japan. For example, 'Message of Rouge' is very popular. It was sung by Yumi Arai.

This movie has many unique characters. For example, Kiki has a cat. His name is Zizi. He can talk with Kiki. But another people can't talk with him. He is very clever and cute cat. This movie tells us," If you believe in yourself, you can do everything."

## Princess Mononoke

*(1997), 133 minutes long, animation, Director and Writer/ Hayao Miyazaki  Stars/Youzi Matuda and Yuriko Isida*

Princess Mononoke has a very deep and direct message. The message is "live". Princess Mononoke is made by Ghibli's writer Hayao Miyazaki. He is one of the famous writers in Japan. He took 20 years to write the movie.

It's time is the far past. Humans infringe on a forest. And gods and animals in the forest is quiver with rage for human's actions. This movie's story plays out against the backdrop of human vs forest. A young man, Ashitaka who had a curse put on him by Tatarigami and a young woman, San, who is deserted by humans and picked up by big wild dog Moro in forest. She is called "Princess Mononoke" they are the main characters. The movie drows Ashitaka and San's encounter and person's grow up through human and forest's battle.

When I watch the "Princess Mononoke", I was just ten years old. This movie is very difficult and scary. But, I can understand the movie is very deep now. So I love the movie. I want to watch the movie for adult. Princess Mononoke's music is very impressive. The music is made by Jyo Hisaishi. My favorite music is "Ashitaka Sekki". The music and movie match each other. I want to take note of it,too. This movie is very grand. You can feel excited and impressed.

# Sen to Chihiro no Kamikakushi (Spirited Away)

*124 minutes long, animation. It was released on 20 July 2001(Japan). Director/Hayao Miyazaki*

Hayao Miyazaki is an internationally acclaimed film director . He also made "Kazeno Tanino Naushika" (Nausica of the Valley of The Wind), "Tonarino Totoro"(My Neighbour Totoro), "Tenkuno Shiro Rapyuta" (The Flying Island of Laputa), and so on. There were so interesting and popular. So, people were interested in this movie. In 2002, it received a grand prix at International Film Festival.

Chihiro, who is the heroine, is 10 years old. She strayed into a strange place to move her family on their way. Her parents has become pigs, and she decided to return them. She meets a mysterious boy named Haku there. She comes to work at a big public bath for the Divine to live and return her parents. She is helped by Haku, and she also gets to grow.

I like this movie very much. First, its mood. The building of various sizes and colors are standing in row. There is peculiar mood. Second, its character. This movie has many characters appear. They are nice. Almost all of this movie's character aren't human. They are like hobgoblins. A frog, a very big baby, a white dragon, etc. They have a lot of mystery, the story is fascinating still.

This is a movie which is popular all over the world. I want you to watch it again and again!

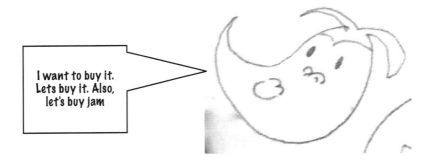

I want to buy it. Lets buy it. Also, let's buy Jam

## Howl's Moving Castle (1 of 2)

*Released 20 November 2004,*
*Writer/Miyazaki Hayao,*
*119minutes long*

A model of Howl's castle made by students at the culture festival

Studio Ghibli made this movie. Each movie which Studio Ghibli made is interesting. The contents are intelligible and the characters are also lovely. Therefore, this movie is popular.

Sophie, a hero, will be able to use magic for the witch of the wasteland, and will be turned into a 90-year old grandma. Sophie who was feeling sad meets with Howl, the magician who appeared at a huge castle which moves. Howl and Sophie live together. War occurred in a certain town one day. Howl went to the dangerous battlefield for Sophie who hates war. Sophie gets to know the life of Howl's things because of magic then, Sophie moves in order to solve (NB understand) the magic used for Howl, and it.

I was impressed seeing this movie. Howl and Sophie are worried about others in it, although they have bitter experience, too. In order to remove others pain, they act with might and main. If I were in the same position, I couldn't imitate it by any means. Therefore, I would like to try hard for me to also get used to like Howl and Sophie.

This movie of Studio Ghibil has various good points since it is very interesting, please see it.

## Howl's Moving Castle (2 of 2)

This movie is the work of Ghibli. the movie which Ghibli makes is popular not only in Japan but also in foreign country.

The characters of this movie are Sophie and Howl and others. Sophie is 18 years old. But she will become an old woman by witchcraft. She was shy but she become cheerful while living with Howl. Howl is a wizard. He is smart and kind. However, in fact, he is weak. These characters venture in the different world from reality.

I like this story very much. Love, growth, and war are drawn on this movie. They help me to grow up. The meaning of living and the wonderfulness of loving someone are known by this movie. Sophie is this movie's character. I like her because she is very kind and cheerful. She makes me happy. And I also like Howl. He is so cool.

Howl's moving castle is an interesting movie of Ghibli.

## Mamosu Hosoda

He is an animation director. Born in September 19, 1967. The chief activity in his films are wholly practical comparative to real life. So we can sympathize with them. His official site said, "It is fantastic, but real." His works are loved by many age groups because there is the work of various genres.

His works are "The Girl Who Leapt Through Time"," "Summer wars", "The Wolf Children Ame And Yuki", "Digimon Adventure: Our War Game", "ONE PIECE: Omatsuri and the Secret Island". They became DVDs and we can buy it.

I watched "The Girl Who Leapt Through Time". It was the first work of Hosoda that I  remember. But I was young, So I hardly remember it. When I was a junior high school student, I watched "Summer Wars". I was a sense of reality. Because he didn't soak a shadow to a character, his work becomes easy to watch in the movement of the character. In addition, he uses the same position many times and traverses. His work has personality, but a good action scene and setting of the character, he introduces information into it with animation and action not words, they have charms to attract many people.

Mamoru Hosoda is an animation director who loved by the wide range of age groups.

## Toki wo Kakeru Shoujo (The Girl Who Leapt Through Time) (1 of 2)

*2006, Director/Mamoru Hosoda, Writer/Takashi Watanabe*

"Toki wo Kakeru Shoujo" is SF movie. A catch phrase is 'the future exists, don't wait'. This movie remade the original after twenty years. It the same that created "Toki wo Kakeru Shoujo" before. Many people loved this movie.

A high school girl in the downtown area of Tokyo, Makoto Konno, one day triggered a grade crossing accident. It awakened the ability to jump in time, to be able to start time again, retro actively in the past Makoto uses wildly her ability when she knows the test problem beforehand gets the perfect score, avoiding being tardy while being troubled at first. One day the relations with two close boyfriends has a delicate change come.

It is a work concerned with Makoto and Chiaki, the relations of three people with Kosuke, mostly. A figure using the ability of the jump for the first time is very impressive. I watched this work too and Wakoto at the time.

It is the youth story in that Makoto, a high school student of develops the ability to jump in time.

## The Girl Who Leapt Through Time (2 of 2)

This movie's director is Mamoru Hosoda. He made this movie and two other movies. All his movie are beautiful and a little mysterious. Many people are absorbed by his movie.

This is a animated movie about a girl. Her name is Makoto. She is a high school student and she is friendly with two boys. Their names are Chiaki and Kousuke. One day, Makoto gets a strange power. It's a power to go to the past. She enjoys her lives with the power. But it has a number of times to go to the past and it worried her. What's more, power's true owner appeared. If you want to know the end, please see this movie.

Every time I saw this movie, I was moved but this movie makes me happy anytime. This movie's images are very beautiful and the story is a little strange. The scene I especially like is their lives at school. I think this movie draws Japanese high school student's lives and a strange world well.

This movie makes me moved and happy, so this movie is popular. I want to many people to see to this movie.

Theater display photo
by chinnian on Flickr

### Summer Wars (1 of 2)

*released on 1st August, 2010 (Japan) Director/ : Hosoda Mamoru, animation , comedy, love story , adventure etc.*

The movie was made by Hosoda Mamoru. He is very popular because he made "The Girl Who Leapt Through Time"

Kenji Koiso , a hero , has Natsuki Shinohara , a senior he yearns for, ask for a part-time job during the summer vacation. The part-time job's contents referred to the fact of "Wanting you to carry out a boyfriend's way." Only at the time of a part-time job period. Since Kenji liked her, he was in high spirits for a while, but the part-time job was quite sublime. I won't give any more away, but it is very recommended.

When I watched the movie, I felt excited. Because I don't meet like the movie in the life. My favorite part is Kenji move to Natsuki . Natsuki go out to Kenji. Kenji is unconscious of it. I tickle to see it.

A catch copy (NB tagline) is "This is a new war."

# Summer Wars (2 of 2)

This movie was created by Honda Makoto, a famous animation director. It was expected by many people thanks to him and the movie is successful.

This movie's teaser is "What connection is our weapon" and this movie's keyword is "family" and "countryside". Also, this movie was screened, around the world, such as in Korea and America. This story's hero is a boy who was not able to be representation from Japan of Math Olympiad. He go to grandmother's house of his yearning senior and he involved in an incident there. Can he solve the incident?

What I like about this movie is the view of the world. I like the gap between human events in the countryside and major incidents in the virtual space of the PC. So I am excited by the movie, I have seen it many times. But I don't get bored at all.

This is a great movie that tells us the importance of ties with the family.

# Umizaru Brave Hearts
*July 13th, 2007 release. CAST : Ito Hideaki , Kato Ai*

It begins with the movie in 2004, the series continues from the serial drama and second movie, and four series item "The Last Message Umizaru" which should have been the conclusion. However, the thought of builders to "have possibilities the theme has was still to convey" whether "we had left it undone " created these movies which were five series items.

It is two years from the previous work. A main character Senzaki Daisuke took a severe duty as an expert "special wrecking crew" of the salvage to engage in the most dangerous case with Yoshioka, the younger student. It was such two, but Daisuke had the second child and Yosioka had the lover of the cabin attendant and sent full days. On such an occasion, while the jumbo passenger plane which lover Mika of Yosioka boards flies toward Haneda Airport, an engine is burnt down, and the flight falls into the difficult situation. A water landing is unprecedented in Tokyo Bay but as dusk approaches it is succeeded in a marine water landing it's only 20 minutes. Can they save all 346 passenger crewmen before the body sinks? You can feel importance of life and the bonds with the person are strong. With a powerful picture to leave you an impression!

I think that how this movie conveys the important messages such as the "life" "bonds with the person" is splendid. It may be thought that this series is ordinary because an ending is a happy ending by all means, but the scene on the way is powerful and I think that I have satisfied enough my seeker.

This movie is very popular because this is the magnificent story that described the growth of a main character and the person who are on the side in, and the corpus from the first movie. I think that this movie conveying many important messages is splendid.

## Brave Story

*Released 2006, 112 minutes, Fuji Television Network, Inc. and Gonzo animation,*

The movie is very popular because the story is interesting and its animation is clean. Fuji Television is one of the most

At Gonzo studios, the makers of 'Brave Story', courtesy of Jyoshiki on Flickr

famous TV companies in Japan. This movie's supervisor is Koichi Chigira, who made many animations. For example, "Detective Conan The Fourteenth Target" and "Mobile Suit Gundam Char's counterattack".

The hero of this story is a boy named Wataru of the fifth grade. He takes a trip that changes his fate in wonderland. There, he meets many friends and grows up.

I like the characters of this story. Wataru is so brave as to go on a trip alone. I cannot do such a thing. Kima who is a creature such as the lizards is a friend of Wataru in wonderland, and he takes a trip with him. Mina who is cat girl takes a trip, too. On the trip, Wataru and they help each other. I think they have the deep friendship which can be born only on their trip. The world that they trip is very wonder. For example, they can use magic there and people who are like an animal live the world.

You should watch this movie to feel an impression. If you do so, you'll surely come to like them. It is a movie to give courage to you. It is popular because the story and characters are very attractive.

Music

Ongaku

音楽

## C-ute

J-pop idols are cute and cool. There are many idol group. Idols can dance and sing. They dance and sing very well. And idols are a good style and good face. We feel fine.

My favorite idol is C-ute. They are very cute. C-ute is five people. C-ute can dance very well. Dance is cute and strange. I like most "Okamoto Tisei". C-ute sing and make me fine. Dance and sing are very powerful. I recommend; "Sekai de ichiban happy na onnanoko". It is girly and cute. MV is very colorful and beautiful.

Idol is young. Young people is very fine. They made us bright. Dance is healthy. Dance is interesting and diet. Because idol is smart. We look like girl's very cute. Fashion is individual. Colorful and short are. I'm happy that I see they. C-ute is osusume (my recommendation).

Idol is cute face, body, voice. Idol group is individual. Idol is Japanese culture. I want to see you Japanese idol C-ute

## Kyary Pamyu Pamyu

Kyary Pamyu Pamyu is a Japanese singer and fashion model. Her name is Charonplop Kyary Pamyu Pamyu. But, her name is so long. So, she is called by everyone Kyary Pamyu Pamyu. She is 19 years old.

*Kyary Pamyu Pamyu in concert courtesy of Guirec Lefort on Flickr*

She was mentioned in the high school book as a reader model when she was a high school student. She also appeared in various fashion shows. Because, she is young and popular, product sales for items which she introduced in the blog were significant.

She made her debut as a singer in 2011. The debut song is "Moshi Moshi Harajuku", and " PON PON PON " in the lead song which has been delivered to the world by iTunes. "Tsukema Tukeru" was released in 2012. This song has been delivered to 23 countries. The result, she won a no 7 position on Oricon Chart ( Japanese Billboard Chart ). From these, she is popular not only in Japan but also in foreign countries.

I think she is very humorous, because she made a costume of stuffed animals and made a candy costume. Her idea is very new. So, I think she is popular. She is unique and has interesting ideas. It is the charm of her.

She has been active not only in Japan but in foreign countries. Her idea is always at the cutting edge of fashion. It will be so in the future I'm sure. I want to support her in the future as a fan.

> Candy, candy. Candy candy, candy

## Momoiro Clover Z (1 of 3)

Concert photos courtesy of dj ph on Flickr

Momoiro clover are idol group. Momokuro is very cute and active.

So we were surprised, because we haven't seen as active an idol group belong to stardust production. They are called "Momokuro, Momokurochan" for fun. Their leader is Kanako Momota.

They released about 20 cd's. Their PVs are original. So they are fun and I am always looking forward to watching it. The average

age of them is sixteen. Ayaka Sasaki is the young of five.

I think Momokuro is one of the most popular idol group in Japan. They do very hard dances are active. So they are different to other idol groups. They sing a surpport song for everyone who does one's best. Many fun times gave a lot of power. They are very powerful and smiley. So our fun always gives us a power. They have a lot of supporter's song to make everyone happy.

## Momoiro Clover Z (2 of 2)

This is a girl's idol group by Kanako Momota, Shiori Tamai, Ayaka Sasaki, Momoka Ariyasu, Reni Takagi. An abbreviated name is Momokuro.It is popular because acrobatic dances including Kanako's jump in which she curves like a shrimp, the music which remains in the head if we hear it once, the figure which sings best. The high-level concert of a fan participatory type. All member's personalities are powerful, and they can make fanny faces. There are many other popular reasons.

Momokuro members are high school students. So they are weekend heroines because they go to school weekday and they work only of weekends. However, Reni works as the everyday heroine because she graduated from the high school.

---

**✻Member's Profile**

*( color / birthday / age / blood type / nickname )*

· **Kanako Momota ( Red / July 12, 1994 / 18 /**

**AB / Kanako↑↑)** Her knack is rhythmic gymnastics, dance, jump which curves like a shrimp. Her charm point is dimples. Her characteristic is the powerful singing voice which strikes the chest.

· **Shiori Tamai ( Yellow / June 4, 1995 / 17 /**

**A / Shiorin )** Everybody's younger sister who is a crybaby and a fawning girl. Shiori is a good eater but slim. Most of the contents of her talk is food. She sleeps well.

---

• **Ayaka Sasaki ( Pink / June 11, 1996 / 16 / AB / ARIN )** Momokuro's idol who is a little sexy and a playful girl. Her knack is puppeteering. Her killer technique is folded arms as if carrying handbag.

• **Momoka Ariyasu ( Green / March 15, 1995 / 17 / A / Momoka )** Her catchphrase is "small giant". Her characteristic is a husky voice. Her talk is long. The king of reaction. The knack, discovered recently is bending a spoon.

• **Reni Takagi ( Purple / June 21, 1993 / 19 / O / Reni-chan )** Her knack is making a funny face. She dances more hard than other members. She is an eccentric girl, so her catchphrase is "electrification girl".

## Momoiro Kuro-ba-Z (3 of 3)

I think the acrobatic dance is one of the reasons for the popularity. But Momoiro Kuro-ba-Z is also an idol group. The second reason is I think that they have unique characters.

Momoiro Kuro-ba-Z is a girl's idol group of five people. The member are Momota Kanako, Tamai Shiori, Sasaki Ayaka, Ariyasu Momoka, Takagi Reni. They have the five colors for their image: red, yellow, pink, green and purple respectively. They always do the best dance in acrobatic dance.

I think that without resorting to lip-syncing to be an idol and to give focusing real song is great. And the best performance to talk in variety shows is great. So I think that it gives energy to those who see it. I have been a fan since they made a major debut.

Momoiro Kuro-ba-Z is a idol group of five people. They do acrobatic dance. And they have unique characters.

## Perfume

It is Perfume, they debuted in 2000, a CD is "released", a group "debutets" They are very cute. They can do

techno pop, electro pop, dancing, singing, talking, etc. And they can do it very well. They are only three girls, but their performance is very powerful.

Contents are music and dancing. The most popular song is "Poririzumu"(Poly-rhythm). We can get them on DVD or CD. It is good balue (value). They have live shows and PVs.

I like them. Perfume is Omoto Ayano, Kashino Yuka, Nishiwaki Ayaka. They are very beautiful and pretty. Their voice differ from other artist. It seems to be techmology. Their dancing also looks like robots. Their movement is refinement in action. Another artist cannot do it. So I want them to make it known in pubric, all over the world. They have a beautiful charm.

## 「Box emotions」by Superfly

*Type : Album, Release : 2009 9/2 Label : Warner Music Japan, Genre : J-POP*

The band that is a solo unit is racing up the charts. She came out and succeeded quickly in the famous musical program after her habit. "Ai wo Komete Hanataba wo" (NB 'Bouquet Charged with Love') a sweet song about beauty and power is her best song.

We can get Courage, impression, and hope from it. The group puts together rock and J-POP. Original music is made. Especially her voice is wonderful. Her hight is short (153cm). However she is powerful, beautiful and has a big voice. So her album is very nice.

I loved Superfly the best when I heard "Ai wo Komete Hanataba wo" And I became a fan! Her song can made your feelings rise.

Because I think she sings with a smile, she sends energy to everybody! Her voice is very wonderful. So your heart will be able to relax and become fine.

## DECO*27

He is a Japanese song writer. His song has very good lyrics. His songs have two patterns. One is cute song ,another one is cool song. So his song is loved by many people.

We can sing almost all of his songs at "Karaoke". He released some CDs. For example "Light lag" and so on. He often used word play in his songs. He collaborated with Koh-Shibasaki and Syoko-Nakagawa. They are Japanese popular singer.

I think he is the best song writer. I like the "Pedal-heart" best in his song. Please listen to his song. I recomend his song. His song makes us happy.

## Kana Nishino

Her name is "Kana Nishino". She is a solo artist of J-POP, 23 years old. Her music is very popular focusing on young men and woman.

She has a lot of fans! It is called "Kanayan" by them. And her music is written about love or friend in many cases. The words of her songs are very straight and gentle. Therefore, it is one of the popular points of hers.

Her style is very good and she is lovely. It is popular about her. Her fashion sense attracts attention not only from fans but also from media. She is not only in music activities but also in magazines, well in many cases. Moreover, in her wonderful place, her songs are words are written for her self.

She is surely writing words still. If she performs a world tour, I would also like to go to the concert.

## Mai Kuraki

I'd like to introduce about Mai Kuraki. She is a singer typify Japan. Do you know her? Some of you may know her because she debut in the U.S with her first song "Baby I Like". Even if you don't know, no problem, I'll tell you. And you will be found of her.

I show about her charm. She has a lot of charm. First is her voice. Her voice is clear and so beautiful. What's more she can sing from high tone to low voice. However, her voice's goodness never lose anytime, so it exaggerate her charm more. Second is her beauty. She is thirty years old now. Though she still keep her the beauty that don't change since she was teenager, she has great charm as a woman. Third is her music sense. She write all the lyrics of her song exclude cover song. Each one of them are including her message. And her singing skill enable it to tell the message in her song completely.

Why I recommend her is because I was moved by her songs. Her songs have different themes. Especially that lave-themed (NB love) is so emotional. Loves what she sing is various. They are positive, sad, complex, and secret. However, each of them have different story and goodness. If you listen to her song, surely you will be touched by it. I think that I want many people to touch her world view.

Mai Kuraki has a lot of charm and talent. Her music will make you impressed. I feel excited, listening her song. I want you to feel like same. Let's listen to and feel Mai Kuraki!

## AAA

They are performance group in Japan. They made famous by producer Komuro Tetuya. He is one of the music producers in Japan. He made many hit music up to now.

AAA has two girls and five boys. Uno, Ito, Nishijima, Atae, Hidaka,

Sueyosi, Urata. They debuted and released their 1ˢᵗ single "BLOOD on FIRE" in 2005. In 2010, they became famous at a burst with 24ᵗʰ single "Aitairiyu". That was produced by Komuro Tetuya. Many people knew AAA then. This year, they will have their 7ᵗʰ anniversary in September.

They not only active group, but also individually active. I think each member has various abilities. So they can take action in many ways. For example, actor, model, radio personality, solo singer and so on. Of course, I love their music make us happy! Their songs have their many feeling. I especially like album is "777"! This album is sold 54,000. This is the first time by them. I expect their action. But I also I have high expectation of each them, too.

Their performance is rising more and more. That is very exciting; especially their LIVE is so good!!

## Arashi

Arashi is a singer group of Japan. The members are five people: Satoshi Ohno, Sho Sakurai, Masaki Aiba, Kazunari Ninomiya, and Jun Matsumoto. They debuted in 1999. First single's name is

*Arashi's own plane, courtesy of suneko on Flickr*

"Arashi". They are working also as actors, not only as singers, and appearing on many dramas.

**Satoshi Ohno** Born-November 26, 1980 (age 31): He is an Arashi's leader. **Sho Sakurai** Born-January 25, 1982 (age 30): He is also a newscaster. **Masaki Aiba** Born-December 24, 1982 (age 29): He is appearing on  a variety show. **Ninomiya Kazunari** Born-June 17, 1983 (age 29): He has experience of appearing Hollywood movie. **Jun Matsumoto** Born-August 30, 1983 (age 29): He is thinking the concert structure in pivot. They are releasing the 39ᵗʰ single and the 13ᵗʰ album now. Moreover, the concert is also held and it can be said that it is a very popular group.

I like Arashi very much, because they are so smart. It comes out in all they do such as a song, performance, and a talk. Moreover, they are very close. It makes us pleasant who watches them. I can feel happy watching them on TV. But, I would like to actually meet them someday. Their songs are good. I like their songs. They sing in a voice that is very gentle to. The singing voice, on hearing it is comfortable. Further, the words are also wonderful. I wish many people hearing their songs.

I think that I want them "Arashi" to become a more popular group, and I want many people to notice the charm which they have.

## 「Time」 by Arashi

*Album Label: Jstorm, release date: July 11, 2007, genre: J-POP*

This album is the seventh one of Arashi. This took first in Original Content Album Chart. Some popular songs are used drama's them songs like 'Love so sweet', 'We Can Make It', and so on. They are in this album. There are each member's solo songs in a limited edition CD.

It has fifteen songs on the regular CD. 'Love so sweet' is a theme song of Japanese drama, 'Hanayori Dango.' This is a sweet love song. 'We can make it' is also a theme song of 'Banbeena' which is Japanese drama, too. This is a cheering up song, and has a rap part. The rap part is made by Arashi's member, Sho Sakurai. 'Rock you' is not a theme song, but we can want to fall in love from it. This song is up-tempo and rap part is so cute.

I love it the best in Arashi's other albums because this album has many songs, for example, a serious song, and a love song. We can look at their many expressions. There are each member's song in a limited edition CD so we can enjoy the whole of Arashi and the individuals of Arashi. If you hear their song, you fall in love!

It's so cool, and cute. Their friendship may give us happiness.

# EXILE

*Debut : 27 September 2001*

EXILE is not an ordinary music group. EXILE gives us not only songs but also love, dream and happiness. "Love, Dream & Happiness", in other words LDH is their motto.

Their performance gives me a deep impression and courage. The reason why EXILE is popular is their way of activity. EXILE is a representative of Japan music artists. It is made up of fourteen people. EXILE's typical example of albums are "EXILE Japan", "Negai no Tou" and "Aisubeki Mirai He". Also their typical example  of songs are "Negai", "One Wish" and "Aisubeki Mirai He". These songs were made for love, dream and happiness. Most of their songs are for future, for children and for all people.

I think that EXILE is the best group. EXILE's live performance makes me happy. I want to aid them. EXILE is a big entertainment group. I love EXILE very much because I like their motto "Love, Dream & Happiness".

# Aqua Timez

Aqua Timez is a music group. It is famous in Japan. Their songs are used for some movies. And, they have broadcast the most famous TV program of music in Japan.

Aqua Timez have operated since 2003. This group is structured with five members now. All of members are men. They sing many love songs. Their voices are a little high pitch.

Aqua Timez made many very famous songs. But, there are many songs that are not famous songs. So, a few people know nothing about this group. When I watched movie, I listened their song for the first time. The song is "Niji". "Niji" means "Rainbow".

Aqua Timez is Japanese famous artist group. I think this group is one of the most wonderful Japanese artists. The song I like the best is "Siori". I love this song. I want you to listen this song.

## Ikimonogakari

Vocalist, Yoshioka Kiyoe courtesy of kimubert on Flickr

Ikimonogakari formed Mizuno Yoshiki on guitar and Yamashita Hotaka on guitar and harmonica on February 1, 1999. Shortly afterward, Yoshioka Kiyoe on vocals joined on November 3, 1999. Genere is J-pop.

They came out with "Sakura" on March 15, 2006. "Sakura" was used as a CM song and Ikimonogakari became popular. They point out people in their song.

They released 24 single CDs, 6 albums and 3 DVDs. Their songs give people happiness. I was moved by the words and they cheered up me. They were awarded a prize of excellence for best picture award and in Japanese records award. People look forward to their songs. "YELL" was set as a piece of national NHK school music competition.

My favorite songs are "Arigato" is the impressive song in which the words of thanks are transmitted through it. "Itsudattebokuraha" has a good rhythm with forward text and song. Other songs are very good song, too. I will become the captive of their songs, all of them, if I hear their songs.

Their music gives people courage and hope. They are excellent artistes.

## 「Arigatou」 by Ikimonogakari

This song was sung by "Ikimonogakari". They sing their excellent song. For example "Arigatou" "YELL" and so on. "Arigatou" became popular because of a drama. The drama's title is "Gegege no nyoubou" , which was released 2010.The drama was hit! so this song would be popular.

We can buy the CD at most CD shops. It is on the album. The

representative lyrics  is "I want to tell you thank you". This song's length is about 6 minutes. It is Ikimonogakari who sings this song.

I like this song very much. This song is filled with gratitude. But, this song CDs is too expensive to buy. I listen to it when I'm disapointed for the result of my exam. This songs makes me hartful and "Try again".

This song would be popular as drama's song. .I think this song is hartful song which I knew.

## Yuzu

YUZU is Japanese singers. This year is 15<sup>th</sup> anniversary.   They are a folk duo. They always have a guitar when they sing a song.   Both of them are 35years old. Their songs are loved by many people!

They made debut in 1998. The debut song was "Natsuiro"(Colors of Summer). It's a popular song for fans. In 2004, they announced the single ,"Eikouno kakehashi" (The Bridge of Glory). It is one of the most famous songs in Japan. It's the theme song of the Athens Olimpics. In 2009, they sold "Niji". It is a CM song of "Nihon seimei" (NB Japanese Insurance company). This song is also a very popular song in Japan. In 2012, this year is the 15<sup>th</sup> anniversary for them. So, they sold a best album "YUZU YOU [2006～2011]".

I think YUZU was a very great singer. Their songs make us happy, and fun. Also, the words of a song make a deep impression to us. I like them very much!!!

# Yui (1 of 2)

She was born in Fukuoka. Her blood type is AB. Her birthday is March 26th. She grew up in a fatherless family. She came out in 2005. Her first song promoted a TV drama on Monday at nine o'clock. She sings feelings for teens. Her most famous song is CHE.R.RY. This song is promoted on a TV CM.

*Courtesy of combpank on DeviantArt*

Her starting point is Street Live (NB. In Japan it is relatively common for musicians to perform on the street, but it is not busking). The music which she made first is "Why me". She is one of the most popular singers in Japan. She not only sings well but also beautiful. She also sings very well in English. So, foreigners will be her fan too.

I like her songs, all of them. I have 20 or more CDs of hers. When I hear her music, I feel healing. What is particularly wonderful is "Simply White". Please hear it once.

She is very cute! She sings very well! Her songs are heart-warming songs.

# Yui (2 of 2)

YUI is a Japanese singer song writer. She was born 1987 March 28 in Fukuoka. When she was a high school student first grade, she decided doing music. She went to Tokyo, and make nice songs in Tokyo. She played the guitar in Tokyo on the road. At first, her songs didn't be listen by anyone. But she has played the guitar, and sings a song. The songs she made for the forts time is "Why me". She has beautiful voice. Her voice got to be called "angel voice".

I like her very much, and listen to her songs everyday. When I god down, I listen to "Never say die" When I was student preparing for or taking examinations, "GRORIA" give me vigor.

# 「guitarium」 by Miwa

*Type: Album, Label: Sony Records, Genre: J-pop, Realese date: March 14, 2012*

The girl is a singer and college sutudent. She does the compatibility of work and study. And, she is 148.9 centimeters tall. So, her cute appearance is popular with younger people.

It's a collection of Japanese pop songs. Miwa has a high and cute voice that young people will like. 'Kataomoi' (Unrequited Love) has a piano that is played by Miwa.

The name of the album combines 'guitar' with 'aquarium'.

I feel in love with miwa when I heard 'Don't Cry Anymore' on TV. I have heard it in live once. I think she is a good role DJ. She is the first girl that made me a fan. The songs make us happy and cheerful. So, if you listen to the CD, you will be captivated by her songs!

## Speed

A music group debuted on August 6, 1996. This girls group are Hiroko Shimabukuro, Eriko Imai, Takako Uehara and Hitoe Arakaki. They were too young when they made their debut. And they weren't only cute but also cool. So they were known by many people soon. They broke up in 2000. But After 8 years, they revived!

*Courtesy of kimubert on Flickr*

They have released 15 singles and 8 albums since 1996. Among their song, "White Love" is popular. The song is Speed's 5th single, which was released in 1997. It's a love song as the name says. Why the song was sold? Because Hiroko and Eriko's singing is very good. Hiroko could utter a beautiful high voice. And Eriko was able to sing fine. Their voices backed up each other. So "White Love" was loved by many young people.

I liked this group when I first heard "White Love". They were cool. My music player is filled up by Speed's songs. Their songs give me energy, but they're not active recently. Their songs aren't more popular than before their breaking up. So I feel a little sad because I know that they were a great group in Japan. I think they can be famous again.

Their songs make you get excited! Please hear the song what is sung by the great girls group, Speed.

## 「Up Sense」 by Mr. Children

*Type: Album    Lebel: TOY'S FATORY Please date: December 1 2010    Genre: Rock*

There are known as a very popular rock band in Japan. They bring about many hits since the 1990s, and the many musicians and celebrities are affected by four people lend by Kazutoshi   Sakurai

is great.

There   are recorded 12 pieces in this album in total. Because the interval between this and the previous works was the longest, this album had a big expection from fans. This album is worth heating because a meaning is put in the text of the music, each one. I came to like Mr .Children because I have heard an album unlike this album last time. And it is, in a sense, like the first album which I heard. Mr. Children makes various impressions on me. I want them to make new music. This CD is a thing of a famous Japanese rock band. If you hear this CD, you feel without usually feeling it.

# Bump Of Chicken (1 of 3)

*Genre: rock, Formation: 1994, Affiliation: TOY'S FACTORY*

I think that their songs are better than other songs of other bands. Of course not only in playing but also the words are very good. Their songs make almost all of people feel. For example, when I suffered one thing, I felt better because I listened to their songs.

The members of BUMP OF CHICKEN are vocal and guitar: Motoo Fujiwara, guitar: Hiroaki Masukawa, bass: Yukifumi Naoi, drum: Hideo Masu. Their major debut song was "Diamond" and their new single CD is "Firefly" September 9 (2012) release. Their lyrics are hard. But I'm sure that you are moved when you understand the meaning of it.

I love BUMP OF CHICKEN. I like all their songs. And they are good looking men. The best reason is that I love Motoo Fujiwara. He is very cool and has a good singing voice. When I went to their live, I was crazy about Mr. Fujiwara. I will love BUMP OF CHICKEN in the future, too.

I think that BUMP OF CHICKEN is the best rock band in Japan, because they are very cool.

# Bump Of Chicken (2 of 3)

They are popular because their songs are used a lot. A main song of drama, video games, and movies. Last year, their song was chose as a theme song of our school festival.

It was formed in 1994. There were four members, and all of them are from Chiba. They were going to the same junior high school. And it was formed in the school festival of junior high school. Their famous songs are "tenntai kansoku" "Karma" and so on.

I think it is one of the most famous hands in Japan. Their music has something what other band does not have. I have not been to live, but I have seen it on TV. It is wonderful. Their music makes "story"

Bump of Chicken is a Japanese rock band, and it is famous because their tunes are often used as a main song, for example, "Sancyome no yuhi" "one piece".

## Bump Of Chicken (3 of 3)

Bump Of Chicken was formed in 1994. It is a rock band of 4 men. The music that they made is very great. They have many fans. For their concert it is hard to get a ticket because it is very popular.

Their music is a story style. It is interesting because it uses a figurative expression. And the melody is very great too. When I listen to it, I am excited. The melody and the text is matched. The voice of the vocalist is good, too. Anyone is impressed by his singing voice.

My favorite of their albums are YUGUDORASIRU and COSMONOTE. It is clogged up with splendid song. Various songs are in it. For example, it has a quiet song and a pop song.

Bump Of Chicken is a splendid group.

## The Bawdies

One of the reasons why they are popular is the vocalist's voice. His voice sounds like a foreign person's one. But he is Japanese.

*Courtesy of missjoeli on Flickr*

The second reason; their songs make us very pleased.

All of their songs consist of English. The roots of their songs is in music black such as Little Richard, Chuck Berry and Sam Cooke etc. The Bawdies consists of four members. All of them are man.

They are child hood friends.

I love all of THE BAWDIES because I love rock'n'roll. Also I like very much their song because it makes me very vigours. So when I feel sad, I listen to their song and dancing turned it around. I love

"SAD SONG" the most of all songs. It has moved many people.

Their song, performance and talks are enjoyed by many people They are popular because they cheer up many people.

## Radwimps (1 of 2)

RADWIMPS is a Japanese four person rock band. An affiliation record company is "EME Music Japan". Affiliation office is "voque thing"

In peculiar voice, since words are also wonderful, it is popular. It was appointed as the then songs of the NHK soccer relay broadcast in the 2011 fiscal year. Relays such as J-League, a primary of the London Olympic Games, besides a domestic tournament and south America in July, are also appointed to use As CM. It excites us.

The words of RADWIMPS, have a deep meaning and we can sympathize. There are also many passionate fans. I think expression of the strength of music is the best . Supposing there is an opportunity, please listen to their music which is an artist very popular in Japan.

## Radwimps (2 of 2)

*Genre: rock  Label: EMI music Japan*

Radwimps's vocalist is Yoziro Noda.  His voice is clear and pure. Everyone is soothed by it. He has written a poem in almost all their songs.  It warmed the heart. So their songs will grip everyone. And the more who hear, the better everyone becomes.

Radwimps was formed by four people.  They are rock band. They debuted in Japan in 2001 and in United states in 2005.  Their debut single was "Moshimo" (If).  It's one hundred yen.  How cheep it is!  They are very popular but have little media exposure. So people who can meet them is very happy!

I heard Radwimps's music for the first time when I was a junior high school student. The words are good and very moving! That was why I started to like it. I always listen to music. Radwimps encourages me. They are encouraging everyone too.

I think nothing is as good a band in Japan as Radwimps. And people who love them is very good.

## One Ok Rock

One Ok Rock is band from Japan. This band is composed of four human. 4th album named "Nice Syndrome" has a lot of cool songs. There is a beauty in the voice of the vocal.

It's a collection of rock songs. Each song has distinctive sound. Especially, "kanzenkankaku Dreamer" is speedy and cool. It has a drum and guitars are matched with the voice of the vocal.

I felt shock and cool to the One Ok Rock when I had listened to this 4th album's songs. I think people who love rock will like. It will be popular with woman face vocal.

Their songs are very cool. Because of the voice of vocal, everyone will like it.

## B'z (1 of 2)

B'z is a music group. Koshi Inaba, a vocalist, and Tak Matsumoto, a guitarist, made it in 1988. The phrases express our mind very well. And the music is fitted with them. These make B'z popular.

Koshi Inaba and Tak Matsumoto work as solo artists, too. I love not only B'z but also Koshi Inaba. Both of them make many songs about love. Their songs always impress me.

Although they are poplar in Japan, they are said that they copied other artists' songs. It may be true. But their songs are so excellent. Some songs make us fine, and others impress us. It may be a little difficult for us to understand their phrases. But they express our minds very well. So, many people were attracted to them. Their live concerts are exciting very much. Of course, listening to their songs of the CD is good. But their performances in live concerts surpass

it. In fact, they are good at speaking English. And they also sing songs in English. Sometimes they have their live concerts in America. I want you to hear their songs, and go to their live concerts.

B'z is one of the most popular music groups in Japan. They are very popular because their phrases of songs make many people sympathize and playing the guitar, singing songs very well.

## B'z (2 of 2)

B'z is a Japanese music group. It's very popular because the songs made by B'z are so cool. Koshi Inaba sings a song, and Takahiro Matsumoto play the guitar. They play the rock music. For example, "ultra soul", "Shoudou" and "Eienn no tsubasa" are known almost all Japanese.

B'z releases a lot of music CD and DVD. They are active since 1998. So they have large amount of songs. The newest their concert DVD, C'mon is expensive, but it's so valuable. And also their music CDs are so nice.

I think they are wonderful. To make a lot of good music like that is very very cool. But they play rock music, so there are some people who unlike it because the rock is for younger. So I want to listen their music only people who was really interested in it.

The B'z is made up of Koshi Inaba and Takahiro Matsumoto. They songs are rock, and those are so cool. Their songs are so famous and so popular. Let's listen to B'z!

# 「C'mon」by B'z

*Released in 2011.*

The band, B'z is the hottest rock band in Japan. They debuted in 1988 and released many CDs. A member of B'z, guitarist, Matsumoto Takahiro plays the ending theme of Japan's most popular music TV program, Music Station.

A CD album 'C'mon' was made in the beginning of 2011. Then March 11, the Great East Japan Earthquake happened and the band had to stop making the album. But they thought and decided to start the work again. A song in the album, "C'mon" contains the meaning of "together" and "love to people around you". It was a strong message to help people after the Earthquake.

I think the song is very nice because the sounds of the guitar and the voice are both wonderful and their combination is beautiful. It is common in all their songs. This song's lyrics are very impressive. It makes me positive.

# 「Magic」by B'z

It is the 17th album which was made by B'z. B'z is one of the most famous music groups in Japan. B'z's members are Koushi Inaba (Vo.) and Takahiro Matsumoto (Gu.). They started band activity as the B'z in 1988. They have tried hard and make a lot of recored. In 21 September 2007, they were elected "**Hollywood Walk** of Fame". They were 176th prize winner, and the first prize winner in Asia.

This album was put 13 songs.

| | |
|---|---|
| 1. Introduction | 8. MAGIC |
| 2. DIVE | 9. Maydai! |
| 3. Time flies | 10. TINY DROPS |
| 4. My lonely town | 11. Dare ni mo ie nee |
| 5. Long time no see | 12. Yume no naka de aimashou |
| 6. Ichibutozenbu | 13. Freedom Train |
| 7. PRAY | |

My most favorite song is 7 track'z music " PRAY ". It was used as a theme song for a movie.

# 「Sicks」 by The Yellow Monkey

*Type: album, Release date: January 22, 1997, Label: Fan house, Genre; rock*

This band started their performance in 1990. They look gorgeous. Their live performance is a legend, and has an effect on young bands. "Sicks" is less gorgeous than any other album. But it is said to be a masterpiece. I guess the album is full of life power.

Track 2,"I CAN BE SIT, MAMA" is a kind of word play Japanese word "Akkan-Be" is almost equal to "I CAN BE SIT, MAMA". Track 4, "Singer song at TV problem" means satire to himself. Track 10, "Flower Storm" is a love song. The song is about breaking off the relationship between a man and a woman.

I feel this album has the best lyric in Japanese music history. I especially love "Tengoku-Ryoko". This song starts only with guitar. That sound is too strong. And sabi, the liveliest part of song, so beautiful. Sabi has no drum's sound. So I feel time has stopped. The last number, "Life's end" is a message for writer's grandmother. The message is full of love and thanks for grandmother.

You may not be able to understand every word of a song, but you can feel THE YELLOW MONKEY's soul.

## GreeeeN

It's a singers group in Japan. GReeeeN is a music group in Japan. The members are four people. The genre of their songs is J-pop. They write the words and composition by themselves. The rhythm and words of their songs are very nice. So, there are many people who sympathize with it.

GReeeeN has worked since 2002. They don't reveal a face to media, because all the members wanted to become dentists and considered its coexistence with medical life. So, they have never appered on a PV either. This thing surprised people. The representative songs of GReeeeN are "Aiuta" and "Kiseki" etc. Then their albums won many prizes. Their songs are loved by many people.

I think that GReeeeN is great. As one of the reasons, when the earthquake happened in Japan 2011,3,11. They started the revival project "Green boys Project". It is a project for encouraging victims. For example, they contributed their song for free. I was impressed when I knew of the project. I thought that the power of music is wonderful!

And I liked GReeeeN more and more. I want GReeeeN to do their best from now on. The music group which doesn't reveal a face to media. Their songs are loved by many people.

I could be Greeeeen, but I'm red and white

# 「Ellegarden Best (1999-2008)」 by Ellegarden

*Type: Album, Release date: July 2, 2008    Label: Japanese punk rock*

Courtesy of kk+ on Flickr

The album is loved by many fans because there are a lot of good songs in the album. Ellegarden is singing not only in the Japanese language but also in the English language. And their English pronunciation sounds clear. They have some songs that are sung in only English. So sometimes I forget that they are a Japanese rock band when I listen to their songs. In addition, they have some songs that are sung in both languages. Two languages make a fresh sound and cool music.

The band is composed of four members. The members are Hosomi Takeshi, Ubukata Shinichi, Takada Yuichi, Takahashi Hirotaka.

"Ellegarden Best (1999-2008)" is a collection of rock songs. And these songs are chosen from their various songs. The album can be said to be *Best of Ellegarden*. "Star fish" has the highest popularity in their songs. I like it too. Its sounds are very catchy. And the words are beautiful. "Supernova" is one of my favorite songs. The song is sung only in English. Although I can't understand all the English words, I like the song very much.

They use Japanese and English. I think this point is very good. Now, it is important to make a global connection. Music can connect Japan and other countries. In fact, K-Pop connected Japan and Korea. In this situation, Ellegarden's songs suit to connect Japan and other countries. I hope their songs will play an important role for this.

This Japanese punk rock band should be known by more and more people.   Please listen to their fresh sound, beautiful words, and global music.

# Sekai no Owari (World's End) (1 of 2)

Sekai no Owari is famous artist group organized 2007. They active in Japan. They came out 2011 August They released 1st album "EARTH" It is very good and sale a lot

Especioury I like "Sekai he Iwa" in the album This song is countained peculiar word. For example,"peace". So they have being popularity artist group

# Sekai no Owari (2 of 2)

They made it in 2007 Sekai no Owari is popular. Sekai no Owari is four piece band. Their music is pop and cute. They are called "SEKAOWA". Sekai no Owari's members are "Satoshi Fukase", "Shinichi Nakasima", "Saori Fujisaki" and "DJ LOVE".

I got the album "ENTERTAINMENT". "ENTERTAINMENT" has 16 tracks.

| | |
|---|---|
| 1. The entrance | 9. "Seibutu ga kutekigen soukyoku" |
| 2. "star light parade" | 10. TONIGHT |
| 3. Fantasy | 11. "yume" |
| 4. Illusion | 12. "Katyoufuugetu" |
| 5. "Fushityo" | 13 ."Honoo no Senshi" |
| 6. "Tenshi to Akuma" | 14. Fight Music |
| 7. Love the warz | 15. "Nemurihime" |
| 8. Never Ending World | 16. "Fukaimori" |

The album is good value with live DVD at"NIPPON BUDOUKAN".

The DVD is very nice. The album is very good album.

Sekai no Owari's songs are very nice. For example, "Nijiiro no Senso" is great music and the words of a song lyrics is extreme. "yume" is very pop and very excite. "Fukai mori" is most violentest in all SEKAOWA music. I feel excite when I listen to it. My heart is very high.

They are new type band. So they are popular. They music makes our happy. "Sekai no Owari" is very nice band.

『Butterfly』 by

L`Arc~en~Ciel

Courtesy of Angelina S on Flickr

"L`Arc~en~Ciel" is a popular rock band in Japan. In March 25th , 2012 , they did a concert in Madison Square Garden in NY ; the most popular arena all over the world . It was the first concert by Japanese band .

This album is the newest their one. It has 11 songs. L`Arc~en~Ciel is a rock band, but in recent years, their songs take in orchestra. Hearing it, I feel good. It`s track list as follows:

| 1, CHASE | 7, DRINK IT DOWN |
|---|---|
| 2, XXX | 8, wild flower |
| 3,Bye Bye | 9, SHINE |
| 4, GOOD LUCK MY WAY – BUTTERFLY ver.– | 10, NEXUS 4 |
| 5, BLESS | 11, Future world |
| 6, shade of season | |

"CHASE" was used as a movie: WILD 7`s theme song. "GOOD LUCK MY WAY" is the first song after the 20th anniversary. And it

My new
friends.

was used as a animated movie: Full metal Alchemist`s theme song. "BLESS" was used as a theme song of 2010 winter Olympic games on NHK; Japanese governmental broadcasting. "DRINK IT DOWN" was used as a theme song of a TV game; Devil May Cry 4. "NEXUS 4" was used as a theme song of a Japanese car maker; SUBARU`s LEGACY.

So, Butterfly has many great songs like this. By the way, I`m certain that "wild flower" is truly a great song. It is written about the 3.11.earthquake. Its lyrics recall to me memories about then. I think they have unique aftertaste.

"BUTTERFLY" has a lot of messages for you from L`Arc~enCiel.

## Acid Black Cherry

Because the vocalist who is named "Yasu" his voice is very high and clear. It always makes us happy.

Their songs are a kind of "Rock", but, it is not hard rock. They have a song "Fuyu no Maboroshi" (Winter's Illusion). It is one of the most popular winter songs in Japan. Last year, this song became No.1 just a winter song on TV but it is used on Count down TV. Count down TV is one of the most famous music TV in Japan. (NB. It's the new year TV show where lots of musical guests perform while waiting for the new year to start)

I want to them to release a lot of songs. I want to listen to their songs more and more. They released about twenty songs. I'm not satisfied with it. I think, they will be able to release around fifty songs!

Acid Black Cherry is one of the most famous rock bands. Their songs are very good. I love them.

## The GazettE

I'll introduce my favorite band. It is " the GazettE ". They are Visual Kei. It is called V-Kei for short. The feature of V-kei is flashy make up, dress, and hairstyle.

The melody is like hard-rock, heavy-metal, pop. There is "Anata no tame no kono inoichi" (NB "My life for you", sacrifice) in their

*Courtesy of ochoresotto on Flickr*

music. It is difficult to decipher, but it is not thing to hearing. It is unique, the words, melody. The inside of the fan is a popular song.

My favorite song is "Hyena". It is hard-rock. The melody is violent and cool, I like ballad. Their and fan's song are "Kareuta". Then I was impressed by them I decided to support them. I can't decide the best song. But, you should hear "Cassis". Because I sounded my mind. Moreover, I cried. They have grown cooler and their songs are better. I'll love "the GazettE" forever!

I am writing much about the GazettE. It was very fun, because I can write about the GazettE.

## ViViD

ViViD is visual rock band. Menber's are Shin (Vo.) Reno (Gu.) Ryoga (Gu.) IV (Ba.) Ko-ki (Dr.) ViViD is so cool, theirs songs gives us happy times and hope.

ViViD's members gathered in 2009, but I didn't knowing them than. 2010 summer, They released a new single "Precious". It was just then that I knew their activity. ViViD's songs are shaking to my heart. I know nobady but them that I fall for in bands. They realize their dream. They sung at Nippon Budoukan (NB A large stadium in Tokyo, the cultural equivalent of Wembly in England) in Junualy 7 at 2012. The total number they have released 11 CDs, 2 DVDs. Now, ViViD is singing the theme song of an animation.

I think ViViD can be a major group more than now. Of course they are already known by many people in many countries, but they will not be setting a cutegory yet. Maybe their name spread all over the world soon. I'm proud of a fact that I love ViViD and theirs fans. Shin's voice is very beautiful. His soprano and performance is healling to my heart when I'm tired and it encourages me. I want to go to a live, but they don't comes Sendai much. That is a weakness. I think ViViD is active in the music world than now. Also I like often visual rock bands.

They often sing a love song. That all songs reach us heart.

# Games
# Ge-mu
# ゲーム

# Sugoroku

Sugoroku is a board game. At edo era (1603-1868), Ban-sugoroku (likes backgammon) and E-sugoroku were called Sugoroku, but now only E-sugoroku is called Sugoroku.

*Courtesy of asobitsuchiya on Flickr*

Sugoroku (E-sugoroku) is one of the games which are like The Game of Life. It needs a picture which has some squares and playing pieces. The picture's squares are places which playing pieces can be put in. This game's most simply rule is, roll the die (dice) and step playing pieces from the "Start" square to the "Goal" square.

It's picture's squares often have something drawn on them: a popular place's name, a part of history, months (often January to December), etc. In this connection, at present, often some orders are written.

Sugoroku (E-sugoroku) is on interesting game. I have two reasons. First, it can be played and enjoyed by young children and elderly people. This means this game can be played with family. I think it's good. Second, because of it's simple rules, anyone can create new Sugoroku. Sometimes someone says "I'm tired of playing this game." But this game is able to create many others, so you can enjoy Sugoroku. (Someone who is tired of creating Sugoroku may not think so.)

It's an old, simple game, but in the other words, It's able to create an interesting game.

## Tamagotchi

It is popular for elementary school children. Because the characters are very cute.

Tamagotchi is a portable game. It can bring up many kind of characters, for example Memetchi, Mametchi and Kuchipatchi. They are electronic pet. We can feed they and enjoy playing a game. It is selling for two thousand yen.

I started playing it when I was a fourth grader. I think it is a nice portable game. Because it is easy to play for young children. But some parents think it is a bad toy. Because we are often too absorbed.

Tamagochi is a portable game released in 1996. It is popular for children because it is easy to play for them and its characters are very cute. I think it is a nice game. I have three.

*Courtesy of xmacex on Flickr*

## Mobage

It is the joint-stock counpany D.N.A in 2006 Febrary. Mobage is the game which can use all Japanese a mobile phone have it. People who began mobage is very much more and the conpany is managing the professonal baseball team.

Mobage`s game is kind of copperates with Japanese Anime and cute character and Mo-Bage`s original and so on. Mobage is not only a game to play but also we can talk in a community circle, making yourself character. In a community circle, there are many title. Food, trip, hobby and so on. You can come and touch Japanese People.

Mobage`s the biggest characteristic is not paying the money which Mobage needs to begin.You can play it with no pay of all. But reality is not sweet. There are "Items" and "Gacha" in Mobage. When we buy them, we must pay the money and we must pay the money to win many times. A result, there are many People who pays much more.

I brgan it 2011[th] Feburary. By the way, I don`t pay the money to play it now. I recommend the Mobage. Because of it is interesting and stoping Mobage`s game is no regretly. Beginning and stopping is not both of paying the money. How about you play Mobage ?

Mobage is many kind of contence and interesting! But be careful nor to pay too much...

## Game Freak

It is the company was started in 1989. Game Freak is one of the most famous conpany of TV games in Japan. They made " Pocket Monster". Pocket Monster was made in 1996.

It became popularity soon and sold 200,000. Now they have sold five titles and the sales of these are over 100,055,000.

Game Freak was started by Taziri and his friends. Taziri Satoshi is Game Freak's president. At first, he is a writer who wrote about TV games in college school. He gathered friends and made a literary cotrie magazine circle. It is starting of Game Freak. After that, he wanted to make a game. He and his friends made a game from independence work. They started the company taking advantage of it.

I like TV games. I like especially the game was made by Game Freak. Why can they made interesting games? Because they likes games truly.

I always look forward to sale of their games. They will delight us through a game from now on.

## Pocket Monsters

*Released 1996, Nintendo*

It is released 21. Red, Green, Brue, Pikachu, Gold, Silver, Cristar, Ruby, Supphire, Emerald, Fire Red, Leaf Green, Diamond, Pearl, Platinum, Heat Gold, Soul Silver, Brack, White, Brack 2, White 2.

A Nintendo Service Center
Courtesy of HeyRocker on Flickr

This first game (Red and Green) was released in 1995. The chilren who played these are adalt now. This games that can be enjoyed by children and adalts.

A boy (A girl) travel to be a Pokémon master. Then he is asked by a doctor in the region. The contents is finding Pokémon which exists in the region, to recordo an illustrated book. This is an RPG travel to various town to get eight badges, bring up monsters. Now more than 600 Pokémon exists.

Regions which each stage is set is actually modelled on Kanto and Kinki, Kyusyu, Hokkaido in Japan, and New York in America. By playing it me can feel its like traveling there a little. Animation has been broud casl-for 16 for years, movie comes on 15th aniversary.

It is a game loved not only Japan but also around the world. This is the game been loved by many people.

## Scizor

I introduce a Pokemon's character "Scizor". Its Japanese name is "Hassamu".

It has appeared in the "Pokemon game" since 1999. It is the character. The body is red. The arm is claws. It has wing but it can't fly. It looks like crawfishes and mantises.

I think Scizor is the most cool and strong character in the Pokemon. Its weak points are few and it has a lot of resistance to another type's technique. The first thing, it has various techniques. So may of Sizor's users exist around the world.

Sizor is popular, because it is cool. It's my partner.

## Hoshino Kirby

Hoshino Kirby was made by Masahiro Sakurai who works at HAL library. His main character is Kirby. His body is all pink and ball. It's so simple that we can write it easily. He's very cute and strong!

*Courtesy of Sodaniechia on Flickr*

It has a game which was made in 1992. This game's story is simple, too. One day, King Dedede who is king of Pupupu Land keeps all the food in Pupupu Land. If this situation continued, people who live Pupupu Land would die. And King Dedede took not only the food but also Kirakira Stare which is Pupupu Land's treasure. So, Kirby started on adventure to recover them.

This story is the first story. Hoshino kirby became a series game. And the story is different every game. When the second game was saled, Kirby had special skill. It's called Copy Ability. When Kirby eat that had something ability, he can use the same thing. For example, he can use sword, become a bird, brow fire breath and break all things.

This game is very interesting. When I played this game, I was used to playing it soon. I think all people can enjoy playing this game.

In 2012, Kirby's game has a anniversary 20th. This game will be loved by many people. Of cause, I will, too.

## Puyo Pop

*Released 1981. made by a stock company "CONPAIRU".*

The game of Puyo Pop Which called "Puyopuyo" in English is kind of puzzle game. It is popular because It can be played so easily. As you play Puyopuyo, all you have to do is know that when four falling blocks which are the same color louch, they disappear. So whoever can play it.

The game of Puyopuyo has been made in ten soft wares. All soft wares have two mode. First, the main mode of Puyopuyo is battle mode. If you strike out blocks called "Puyo", The disturbance blocks are sent to enemy's area. And players whose area fills up with block is defeated Another one is called "Tokopuyo". You play it alone and try your best score. In this mode, the falling blocks became faster and faster.

You can buy this game at a store which sells many games. In my opinion, I have four games in the Puyopuyo series. So I have played this game for twelve years. Certainly, I like it very much. However, I don't recommended it to my friends, because there is a difficult and complex technic if you want to enjoy this game really. It is called "Rensa". It means links. It takes a long time to master it. Frankly speaking, some people don't feel Puyopuyo interesting until they get used to handling it.

That's the difference between tetris and puyopuyo and why this game is not as popular as tetris.

I think Puyopuyo is popular because it has depth. And I want more people to obsarb Puyopuyo.

## Monster Hunter

Monster Hunter is a hunting action game that was released from the company CAPCOM. The sequel was released for the first time since a lot of it has come out in 2004.

There are many different types of monsters and weapons, none of them are cool. In addition, it is that a biggest reason is that you can enjoy with your friends in co-op. Joy when you beat together the powerful monster is exceptional. Not have to be good at their example, as it will help everyone, story will not proceed.

This game, so that you can enjoy even one person, please try to play us.

## Monster Hunter Portable
*Released 2010, PSP game, CAPCOM*

CAPCOM has ever also made "Street Fighter" and "Packman". The reason why it is popular is that it can enable us to play with our friends, so we can help each other and it helps us to clear a quest.

*Character Cosplay courtesy of MiNe on Flickr*

You are a novice hunter who comes to Yukumo village. You see a monster which looks like a wolf. You are damaged by him. So you swear to get revenge on him. Now, your hunter life begins.

It may suit beginners best because it is not so difficult. So you can enjoy it if you have never played "Monster Hunter" series. It is the game which accuses reality. So it takes us long time to hunt monsters but you can feel a sense of achievement. By the way, my favorite Monster is "Diablos"

It is the game which you can enjoy alone or with friends.

## Dragon Quest

Because it is a very simple game, anyone can enjoy himself. It is very cool and interesting after all. It is an RPG called "Dragon Quest" Although a tale changes with different games, It is the story that

*Slimes courtesy of Pete Barr-Watson on Flickr*

a hero beats the devil fundamentally. A hero meets friends through an adventure, grows up mutually, and fights with demons. It takes about 50 hours to finish the game.

I would like to see a new story in the game. Cooperating with friends and beating a strong demon are very exciting things. And a hero and friends grow as it approaches in the end of tale. It is also interesting thing that his arms become powerful and powerful mystic words also use memorized by them. It fights with in the end.

Probably, there is no person of Japanese people that do not know it, easily because a cute devil called "SURAIMU"(NB. Slime) appears in the game. Please do it and fight with "SURAIMU"!!

## Little Buster

*PC game, Released: July 27, 2007, Genre: Love Adventures*

"KEY" which was a famous company made this game. Beside, the character is individual, and the voice actor is more excellent, too .The reason why this game is popular is innumerable.

Character figures courtesy of Antonio Tajuelo on Flickr

This game is a love adventure. A player becomes a chief character and solves some problem to happen in the game. I fall in love with one of seven girls when I solve the problem. For example, heroine fights against darkness of the mind, I help her when she becomes killer .It is a game with such friendship and love.

I like games. Above all, the love simulation is particularly good. Because, it is something we can experience that we cannot experience by our selves. This game can feel not only love but wonderful friendship, and comes, the feeling that the hero and friends think mutually that they are important .This is impressed very much.

The theme of the game is "friendship". Therefore it is unusual for such a game. A big characteristic is it is individual, and a lot of male characters of the leading grade appear. In addition, the prominent gag all zeroed in the life of the abdominal muscle of player.

## Inazuma Eleven Series

Inazuma eleven. Inazuma eleven 2 (fire/blizzard), Inazuma eleven 3 (challenging for world spark/bomber/the orge), Inazuma eleven GO (sine/dark) are games and animations. First game released on 1 July 2010 presented by "revel five"and "TV Tokyo"

Inazuma eleven ⇒ Mamoru Endo lives in Raimon city loves soccer very much. But he's school haven't soccer club. He makes a soccer club and aims at the top of Japanese junior high school student.

2 ⇒ They become top of Japanese junior high school student. Then, they attacked their town by using soccer. They ran around the Japan to save the peace.

3 ⇒they could save Japan's peace. They aim at top of world. In side story future people attacked their past.

GO ⇒ 10 years later Soccer is controlled. Tenma Matukaze, new student of Raimon junior high school. He changed that system and people around him.

This story and game are over dimension soccer battle. In story they found very good friend around oneself and important for never give up. We can watch they bond. But this is over dimension soccer battle. They meet maney things (shoot is burning, fighting a being from outer space, fighting future person). Some people can't understand this. And may be dislike because that is too far away from reality.

Endo Mamoru loved soccer. He make strong his team and bond with his friend.(1~3) Matukaze Tenma changes his team and many people by his play. They found a lot of important things through praying soccer.

# Touhou Project (games)

*Released 1996, creator/Junya Ota.*

These games are mainly shooting game. Any people call it "Curtain of fire game". It is not uniquely easy these days, and it has very wonderful back ground music. So, many people who were charmed by it buy it and play them.

We can play it with a computer. It is a coterie game. But it is hardly different from popular games. We can play it on PC only. We use a keyboard to play it. The operation of the games is simple. For example, moving is with arrow key, shooting is Z key. It has four difficulties: Easy, Normal, Hard, and Lunatic. Lunatic is harder than other difficulties.

I have liked these games since I played it, because these games are not only that the operation is easy, they have the scenario which is set up exactly and characters with individuality. Most characters are women, but they are pretty and fun. These games have a lot of BGM, too. They are very beautiful and wonderful. My mind is moved only to listening them. These games are very, very exciting.

The operation, scenario, characters, BGMs, there are these wonderful things in Touhou Project. Playing it will give you good time.

Cosplay courtesy of Luciius Kwok on Flickr

# THE PEOPLE WHO BROUGHT YOU THIS BOOK ARE:

## The students – our writers
We students of Sendai Mukaiyama Senior High School, Miyagi prefecture Japan are all 16 or 17 years old, boys and girls studying hard to pass college entrance exams. Most of us enjoy English and we were excited to have this chance to tell the English speaking world about our favorite things in Japan. We hope you enjoyed this book and that you start to see how wonderful Japan is! Please learn more and visit Japan in the future. We welcome you.

## 2nd grade Japanese teachers of English – our project organizers:
Mr. Endou
Ms. Okuma.

## Japanese Teachers of English – our project consultants:
Mr. Otomo
Mr. Takahashi
Mr. Sakuma
Mr. Maruyama
Mrs. Sugawara.

## ALT/Native English Speaking Teacher – our project creator, editor and publisher
Matthew Rowe. He is from the UK and has 6 years experience of teaching (4 years TEFL). He also is an author with two self-published titles that gave him the technical knowledge to produce this book . In his spare time he manages and is the co-founder of *Sakura Panda Tea Time,* a Japanese culture blog and video series created with the goal of informing foreign people about Japanese culture in as odd a way as possible.